ROOTS and WINGS

Life's Lessons in Aphorisms

Balu Athreya

Roots and Wings: Life's Lessons in Aphorisms
Balu Athreya

First published in the United States by
Nicasio Press
Sebastopol, California
www.nicasiopress.com
Printed in the United States of America
ISBN 979-8-9897756-2-0

This book is dedicated to the future generations.

CONTENTS

PREFACE

This book is dedicated to the future generations, inspired by a famous quote attributed to different sources: "There are only two lasting bequests we can hope to give our children. One of these is Roots; the other, Wings."

The "Roots" come from one's family, society, culture, and traditions, practiced with respect and humility. The "Wings" come from an open mind that respects other's traditions and points of view.

The primary goal of the book is to point to science and spirituality as the unifying forces of the world since both aim for universally acceptable and useful truths. In these aspects, science and spirituality are the wings. At this time of climate crisis and information disorder, we need combination of scientific methodology and philosophy to understand the external physical universe, and the wisdom of Eastern and indigenous philosophies (theories of the Upanishads, practical approaches of Buddhism, and creation myths of the indigenous systems) to understand the inner, spiritual universe. The book includes both.

I have thought and written about the issues discussed in this book in my personal blog site and in my seminars for over ten years. These are based on my personal life journey as a physician, born and raised in one culture and influenced by higher education and life in another culture. I was influenced by Eastern and Western philosophies and scientific training.

I have had many teachers—family members including my children, grandchildren, friends, patients, and their families. The number of scholars and teachers from the past who influenced my thinking are too numerous to count. My special thanks to all of them.

I was fortunate to show an initial draft of the book to Mr. Ed Levy, an experienced editor. The current format of expressing my thoughts in the form of aphorisms was his suggestion. I wish to thank him for spending his time with me and making several suggestions.

Finally, my thanks to Laura Duggan of Nicasio Press for her enthusiastic support in getting the book published. Her background in philosophy, particularly Indian philosophy, was extremely helpful in my revisions.

May all be well! May all be safe! May all be free from suffering! May there be peace and harmony!

INTRODUCTION

Dear Asha, Ajay, Ravi, Ariana, Roma, and Sai,

I am writing this book summarizing my thoughts on my most favorite topics for meditation as if I am writing just for you, my grandchildren, as a personal note. But this is meant for all the grandchildren of the world. I know that these topics are philosophical, and you may not get to them until later in life. That is fine. But I hope you will get to at least some of these essays.

During a group discussion I had with all of you recently, I realized that children of the future are increasingly likely to be global citizens, migrant and mixed, not tribal, nor tradition-bound, who value both science and indigenous knowledge, and who value both religion and spirituality. I also know you will be living and working in an increasingly technological world. You may even be living in a world of cyborg with robots run by AI. Therefore, you will have to learn to use technology wisely for your survival.

Your world is also likely to be removed farther from Mother Nature. Religions will probably play a lesser part than spirituality in your lives. I remember one of you asking what spirituality means. I remember being asked questions such as "Why should everyone marry?" and "Why should we bring in more children to this chaotic world?"

I do not have good answers to your questions. I am glad you are asking them. But you have to think deeply on your own about these questions with an open mind and humility. I hope we have given you an adequate knowledge about your "roots" and given adequate freedom to sprout your own "wings" so you can reflect on such important questions.

This is a book containing personal philosophy based on my reading of Eastern and Western philosophies, experiences in my professional life as a pediatrician, and personal reflections. Obviously, not all the ideas are original insights. In my work as a physician, philosophical thinking opened my mind to understand events in people's lives. It helped me develop my own values to guide my personal and professional lives.

My roots in India and my professional training and career in the US gave me a perspective on the strengths and weakness of the values and philosophies that underpin the structure and function of these two cultures. The values in Eastern philosophies come out of thinking of individuals as part of the whole, everything in this universe as imbued with spirituality, time as cyclic, and logic as dialectic. The values in Western philosophies come out of thinking of individuals as the centers of focus, emphasis on the context, Aristotelian logic, and considering time to be linear.

In addition, the word *knowledge* is generally considered as knowledge about the observable universe and this world—worldly knowledge. But knowledge is not just scientific knowledge based on objective evidence. It is also knowledge of lived experience, subjective knowledge, and indigenous knowledge. The word for knowledge in Sanskrit is *gnana* (or *jnana*) similar to the Latin *gnosis*, which includes knowledge of this knowable universe as well as of the unknown and the unknowable, which may be considered spiritual knowledge.

Scientific advances made possible by the Western philosophies and methods with their roots in ancient Greece have benefitted the entire world. Scientific method requires breaking down the whole into parts and studying the particular in detail. This makes it difficult to reconstruct the whole from an understanding of the parts. Scientific method tends to ignore useful knowledge acquired from experience. Technological advances made by possible by scientific methods have come with their own weakness resulting in the current crises in the climate, species disappearance, and self-destructive human behavior.

This may be a suitable time to borrow ideas from Eastern philosophies, which are more tolerant of various points of view, more inclusive, and more adaptive to local contexts and conditions. Just as science and spirituality are needed to live harmoniously in the new world, strengths of Eastern and Western philosophies can be combined to create a more harmonious world for our future generations. This is the main purpose for my writing this book.

Let us use science and spirituality like we use the close-up lens and the wide-angle lens of a camera. We need both to get a fuller picture of the world and of the universe. As pointed out by Frank Wilczak, in his book *Fundamentals—Ten Keys to Reality*, complementarity principles coming out of quantum physics have utility in thinking about life on this planet. We are wrapped in dualities both inside and outside. Depending on the perspective, what we observe seems to have different and often contradictory properties—like music as melody or harmony. Looking at the world from different points of view is likely to offer us a better understanding of nature and greater enjoyments in life.

Philosophers from different civilizations have dealt with mighty questions over the history of civilization. Their fundamental questions led to the development of theology initially and later to science. It started with basic questions with consequences in everyday life. It was practical. As more questions about the universe in which we live and about nature were answered through empirical evidence and scientific methods, what used to be called philosophy became an academic discipline in the West. Fundamental questions on the structure and nature of reality became part of what is called metaphysics, which together with logic, epistemology, and ethics is now part of modern-day philosophy.

However, philosophy is not just an academic discipline. It has practical value to give us ethical directions and noble values to lead a compassionate, useful, and fulfilling life. Some of the questions asked by sages and philosophers from the East and the West for practical aspects of living are universal perennial questions:

Who am I?

What is the Universe?

How did it come about?

Can something come out of nothing?

Now that "I" am here, what am I supposed to do?

What is Life? Why?

What is the meaning of life?

Can one live after one is dead? How can that be?

What is a soul? Is it real or a concept we created?

Did a God create the Universe? Or did we create a concept of God to explain the unexplainable?

Whether the first causeless cause is a God or Abstract "That" or "It" or a Big Bang, what was there before?

If the Big Bang caused the universe to expand, where did it expand into?

If I believe in the Big Bang, should I also expect a Big Crunch? (This is a quote from Rev. Thich Nhat Hahn)

When I think I know, how am I to be sure?

What is Awareness? What is Consciousness?

And several more questions of practical importance. For example: What if I do not want to think about any of these questions? How can I lead a useful, ethical, and compassionate life?

These are fundamental questions. Difficult to answer.

There may be, and indeed there are, several answers to these questions. A lifetime is not adequate to read and think about them.

Reflections on these questions led me to some insights that I wish to share. These essays do not address all the questions listed above. But they include essays expressing my ideas from a non-traditional point of view, essays that synthesize different points of view, and essays with ideas, some of them controversial, which I believe will be beneficial to you as well as to future generations. Some of the essays in this book have been published already in my blogs or self-published books, and I have also added a few new ones. These essays reflect my interest in giving equal access to science and spirituality in my thinking. They come out of my desire to synthesize what I have learnt using both Western-style formal logic and the dialectic reasoning of the East.

The book is organized into three sections, namely Science, Spirituality, and Society. However, there will be significant overlap since my intention is to use science and spirituality as a good photographer will use two different lenses for two difference purposes.

Since the essays were written at different periods of time, they lacked flow and coherence. Therefore, I decided to write about my personal experiences that influenced me in my philosophical views and weave them into the three sections to give some context and flow. The subject matter of each essay is given in the form of an aphorism as the title for the essay/chapter. This is a well-known format in the ancient writings of

India such as the *Yoga Sutras* of Patanjali and the *Brahma Sutras* of Vyasa.

My experiences of growing up in India in my formative years including childhood in a village and college years in a big city gave me the "roots." My years spent in the United States, training in pediatrics first and then working for over fifty years in academic medicine (which means taking care of patients, teaching, and research) gave me the "wings." In addition, several remarkable individuals in my life—including family members, teachers, mentors, patients, and their families—influenced my thinking. There were, of course, several books and articles, listed at the end of the book, which also gave me "wings" to take off.

Your generation is facing major decision points that will determine the direction of the future civilization. Earth's resources are being depleted at unsustainable rates and human wastes are drowning the oceans. Several socio-economic factors, fueled by social media, are making the collective behavior of people irrational and self-destructive. You will be living in a world in which humans will have to interact with AI-driven robots capable of making not only major decisions but also executing them on their own. Human involvement in such decisions are imperative since AI cannot make judgements and has no emotions or values. Therefore, you and your cohorts will have to take control and work collectively to define human values that would direct machine-human interactions and the future of civilization.

I hope you will have an open mind and reflect on questions and values that can guide the future of humanity. I hope all of you will use science and spirituality, Eastern and Western philosophies, the mind and the heart, in your personal and professional lives and develop values to live by in the future world of "man and machines."

I hope some of my thoughts in the following pages will be of help in your efforts to improve the quality of life of all the people and all forms of life on this planet. Although I organized these essays under different sections, they can be read at any sequence. They are meant to give you both the "roots" (traditional knowledge, scientific knowledge, and values) and the "wings" (imagination, curiosity, and creativity).

Roots and Wings

Part I. Science

I grew up in India at a time when colleges and universities did not emphasize basic research. The general philosophy at schools and colleges was dominated by emphasis on and complete obedience to the authority of the teacher and on memorization. No one taught logical and critical thinking. We were not allowed to question the statements by teachers even when we knew he or she was wrong. This was part of the culture. This was true even in medical colleges.

I grew up in a culture in which respect for and obedience to elders was expected and indeed demanded. Questioning elders and teachers was considered disrespectful. Initiative and curiosity were not encouraged. If anything, they were stifled, although there were a few bright spots and noble teachers. Indeed, my primary reason for coming to the Unites States for training and later to settle down was my need for "academic freedom."

In my view, we respect age and experience too much in Indian culture. Teachers demand strict obedience to the detriment of intellectual growth. In my view, it should be possible for the younger generation to respect age, experience, teachers and at the same time have adequate freedom and support to express their curiosity and explore new avenues. It should be possible to disagree without disrespect.

At the time I was growing up In India, life ran on faith and acceptance of one's position and status. People accepted diseases, death, and disabilities passively, as part of life, a consequence of past karma. Medical science was not that advanced in the early 1930s and '40s. Even what was known was not available in our town. There were only two doctors in town, and one of them was out of reach for most common folks. Midwives and pharmacists (called compounders in those days) were the primary care providers. Most of us received home remedies for most illnesses. Ayurvedic help was easily available.

Most of us believed that diseases were the acts of "angry gods" and superstitious beliefs were common as they were and still are in many societies. For example, a common remedy families practiced in severe malnutrition was to kill a toad, put it in a bag, and hang it around the neck of the child. Smallpox, which was rampant in those days was attributed to the wrath of a goddess called Mariamman. Of course, there were folks (like the shamans) who could help appease these gods and ward of evils.

The society accepted life's events as inevitable and did not have the mindset to think that it was possible to control diseases or mitigate the effects of natural disasters. The modal behavior was one of "living under nature."

The emphasis on memorization in education had both positive and negative aspects. We were expected to memorize multiplication tables from 1 to 20. We were expected to memorize prose and poetry in more than one language—our mother tongue and English. This emphasis on memorization dates to the Vedic period in India (1,500 BCE), before the advent and use of written language. Even now there are several individuals in India who can recite entire Vedas from memory. It is, of course, a great strength.

Emphasis on memory is a good thing. But the problem is the absence of learning how to learn and how to use what we learnt. Even the examinations were based on testing one's memory and not ability to apply what one learnt. I thought that brain was used as a filing cabinet. I do not know what the current scene is. But that was the way it was.

I arrived in the United States in 1958, soon after the report by Vannevar Bush and his team[1] on the importance of science for technological advances and for improving the life of the people. There was great emphasis on science and scientific research, particularly in medicine and biology. Young investigators were able to get financial support and recognition for their work. The National Science Foundation was established in 1950, NASA in 1958, and the National Institutes of Health expanded in its breadth and scope.

The general attitude was like the slogan of US Armed Forces during WW II, namely: "The difficult we do immediately; the impossible takes a little longer." Scientific research and scientific method were considered the most effective paths to understanding nature and for human welfare. With that attitude, scientific enterprise thrived with breath-taking advances in biology, medicine, physics, chemistry, and so on.

Fortunately, I was able to get my training at the Children's Hospital of Philadelphia, one of the foremost children's hospitals in the US and with great emphasis on research. The research atmosphere was exhilarating, and therefore I spent five years in research after training as a clinician. Later, during my professional life also, my life included research all throughout my career.

I should also point out how different the learning atmosphere in US was compared to that which I experienced in India. The emphasis was on learning how to learn and on problem solving and not just memorization of facts. The

---

[1] Vannevar Bush, 1945

relationship between the student and teacher was almost like that of friends. It was so easy, casual, and informal, I initially thought students were disrespectful of their teachers. We were supervised but were allowed to ask and explore. We were given increasing responsibilities with senior trainees helping the junior ones.

Strengths and Weaknesses of the Scientific Method

My experiences during my post-graduate education and work in the United States helped form my point of view on the strengths and weaknesses of science and technology. These ideas were balanced by my experiences growing up in India. Although great scientists existed both in the East and the West since the dawn of civilization, a systematic approach to scientific investigation came primarily from the Western civilization.

Systems and methodology of science developed in the West have contributed enormously to our understanding of the world we live in. The strength of science is in trying to understand nature by breaking the whole into parts; analyzing and measuring them; developing hypothesis to explain facts and variations; and verifying them empirically.

The weakness of science is its method of breaking the whole into parts and studying the parts hoping to get a grasp of knowledge of the whole. But as Jim Henson, creator of the Muppets, is reported to have said: "When you peel an onion, you have a whole lot of peels and no onion." Whitehead called it "the fallacy of misplaced concreteness."

This is not to say that scientific method is wrong or should be abandoned. It is to point out that the information obtained by scientific method is incomplete and should be supplemented with lived experiences. The whole cannot be understood for what it really is in the real world by knowing all about its individual parts. There are two examples I can draw on: one is about the rose, the beautiful, fragrant flower; and the other is human communication.

The rose is a beautiful flower. Its color is so unique that the name itself stands for a certain color. Its fragrance is unique. Rose honey and rose extracts add unique tastes to food. Rose has romantic connotation, which poets, writers, and ordinary people use to express love. All these aspects of rose cannot be appreciated by knowing the flora and fauna rose belongs to or which essential oils give rose its special aroma, although those pieces of information are of extreme practical value.

The other example is language that we use to communicate. Whorf refers to speech as "the best act man puts on." Speech implies language. In science, language is broken down into sound waves, morphology, phonemes, syntax, semantics, semiotics, etc. We need all these categories to understand speech and language from an objective point of view. But by looking at the parts of speech, we cannot understand speech and language in its full dimension as part of human civilization.

By emphasizing objectivity, science tends to ignore subjective and experiential knowledge. By emphasizing measurement, it creates pseudo-sciences that measure qualities such as empathy, quality of life, and happiness by giving some value in numbers. Qualities that cannot be measured such as love, wisdom, and goodwill are in the backseat.

In addition, one current view of the purpose of science is to "explain, predict, and control." This view is consistent with the current age of technology and our tendency to solve all problems with newer and newer technologies. We forget that every technology comes with its own set of problems. There are times when we must alter our human behavior instead of looking for newer technologies.

When I reflected on the differences in approach to solving problems with scientific reasoning in the West and reliance on faith and tradition in the culture I grew up in, I realized that cultural differences in approach to the world, and the people and even to the cosmos played a major part.

Cultural Differences in Scientific Attitudes

As a pediatrician coming from India, I knew that I should understand the customs, beliefs, and values of the people of the United States to be an effective physician. When I was reflecting on the cultural differences between the Indian culture I grew up in and the American culture I entered in 1958, I stumbled upon a book with the title *Mirror for Man* by Clyde Kluckhohn. I also happened to attend a lecture in Boston on illness-behavior in three different ethnic groups. These both exposed me to the idea of cultural anthropology and to an understanding of differences in cultural behavior.

The book and the lecture taught me a great lesson, which has influenced my thinking for the past fifty to sixty years. I learnt that different cultures approach different stages of life and different events in life from different modes. There is what is called modal behavior for each culture, which means an attitude towards an issue most of the people in that culture take. It is not to be judged as good or bad. It has to be understood in the context of why that custom or behavior developed as well as its advantages and disadvantages.

With that cultural anthropological approach, Kluckhohn-Strodtbeck model suggests that five existential beliefs influence individual choices in every culture[2]. They are:

---

[2] Nolan Weil, 2017

1. Relationship to nature
2. Relationship to human nature
3. Relationship to time
4. View of human actions
5. Relationship to others

There are only a limited number of ways a society and its culture can deal with these beliefs. For example, a culture can live in fear of nature, "go with the flow" and live with nature in harmony or live over nature.

In the 1960s, I thought that the American culture believed in living "over" nature. This drove the engine for science and technology. The culture believed that it is possible to control diseases. That gave the stimulus for investigating the cause for infectious diseases and development of vaccines. That was the stimulus for looking into the causes of congenital malformations and genetic diseases and the elucidation of the structure of DNA. Such research efforts are not likely to thrive in a culture that believes that diseases are due to divine intervention or past karma.

What is the disadvantage of living in the mode of controlling nature? Nature is not fully predictable. There are aspects of nature that just cannot be controlled. Take for example, death. I noticed that people in the West suffered more when someone in the family died. This is understandable given that the culture views time as linear and believes in controlling nature. In such a culture, death is considered final and a failure of human effort. In the East, death is part of life and not end of life; time is cyclic and there are re-births. Grief is tolerated better in the Eastern culture. Additionally, the extended family system is a better buffer for grief than the nuclear family arrangement in the West.

To give another example, relevant to some of the essays in this book, there is a study of child-rearing practices in different cultures. In the US, I found that children were raised from the beginning to be independent. Indeed, in some situations such as toilet-training and adolescent issues, I thought the push for independence was too fast.

This, of course, was and still is dramatically different from the culture I grew up in. Indian culture expects respect for authority and age and obedience to elders. It makes the children dependent on elders and teachers for too long a period. It has its advantages, of course. But so are many disadvantages, such as when the older married children have to follow what their elderly parents and grandparents want them to do. In the workplace, undue respect for seniority throttles innovation and progress.

Cultural attitudes to science can and do change over time. The American attitude to science in 2023 is different from the attitudes prevalent in 1958 when I came to the US. The changes have been dramatic. After a period of dramatic growths in science and technology in every field, we are now in a period of denial of science. Anti-scientific sentiments are influencing education, policy making and public health.

With these thoughts in mind, I share my thoughts on Life, Matter, Information, and Time in the following section.

1. Information is a fundamental unit of nature.

Since information technology is considered the third major industrial revolution, and since information-transfer is crucial in biological sciences also, I am starting with my musings on information.

Matter, energy, time, and space are the basic units of the physical universe. When you add "life" to the universe, awareness becomes an additional essential element. Awareness implies being aware of something. Awareness is conscious cognition of something inside of us or outside. There is a whole new field of biology called basal cognition, which says that every cell in our body has its own awareness. Even single-celled organisms have a sense of awareness in the form of sensing the environment, remembering signals, and responding appropriately for their own survival.[3] This awareness is information about the environment and of signals from within any organism and is crucial in biology.

Therefore, I suggest that we add Information as the fifth basic element of the universe that connects the other four. Physicists have been saying this for several decades.

For purposes of this discussion, I define information, as applicable to biology, as code for complex structure (or organism) or a potential message for a future event. The first portion of this definition relates to space and the second part to

---

[3] Levin, 2019

time. This follows one of the definitions of information in modern terminology, in which information stands for a message, a code, or an instruction.

This definition of information is different from the ordinary meaning of information as part of human communication, where a conversation between two individuals is transfer of information. This is an exchange of information between two entities existing at the same time.

There is another kind of information applicable to biology as instruction, inherent in matter as potential for a future event. This can be transmitted through matter instantly or later. For example, a plant growing out of a seed or milk becoming butter. Information as a genetic code must be present in the seed for it manifest as a tree. Potential for butter must have been present in milk for it to appear under certain conditions. This used to be the area of metaphysics and philosophy, but quantum physicists are now studying it deeply.

When all the complexities are stripped away, the basic elements of the universe are interconnected and interdependent. Matter and energy go together. So do space and time. Life and consciousness (content of consciousness is information) go together.

In the relationship between mass (of matter) and energy in a space-time continuum, they are interchangeable. We also know that everything at sub-atomic level exists indeterminately as a particle and/or a wave-field.

The next pair is space-time. Even without a knowledge and understanding of the space-time concepts of Einstein, we know that there is space even at an atomic level. There is a vast amount of space between the nucleus and the electron orbits, however narrow that may be. It also implies time for any movement to take place through space, however wide or narrow that may be.

That is in the field of physical universe. This idea is applicable to biology also.

In biology, information is the absolute basis of life and is fundamental to reproduction through DNA and genes, the exchange of energy through breath and metabolism, the exchange of information with the external world through the senses and mind/brain functions, internal messages delivered through chemicals and hormones, and the maintenance of integrity of the physical self through immune functions. In short, information is the fundamental unit that maintains all vital functions in equilibrium.

Life depends on energy exchange, which depends on the sun. Life cannot exist without energy exchange. At a basic level, life is an energy exchange. Energy exchange is used to convert information from one substance (matter) into another.

A living organism maintains its integrity and exists at an enormous cost of energy. That energy, obtained from the sun, is used to maintain order in the structure and function of the organism. Left to itself, and without an external source of energy, the body will disintegrate into disorder or chaos (in thermos-dynamic language, it is called a state of zero entropy).

Physicists have been exploring the link between information and energy for the past several decades. The source of information is potential information, inherent in matter. This becomes actualized information, or a different matter, with the help of energy, as pointed out by von Weizsäcker.[4] Physicists consider information as inherent in matter for energy to act on. Information drives energy to act on matter, and it is intimately connected with matter just as energy is. To quote

---

[4] von Weizsäcker, 2006

Seth Lloyd:[5] "To do anything requires energy. To specify what is done requires information."

When space and time are added to these interconnections, this concept of physics is applicable in biology and to the concepts of life and consciousness.

All living creatures are capable of being conscious and aware. As mentioned earlier, even single cells exhibit a sense of awareness (called basal cognition). They all react to the environment to survive. This is possible only if there is a receiver and a responder. This is awareness at a fundamental level. Awareness is information exchange, dependent on energy exchange. Without awareness and ability to respond to internal and external signals, life cannot exist.

Enter higher life forms and human beings with their special brains and mental capacities. Their awareness is different. Their brains are capable of meta-awareness, an awareness of awareness. The highest form of awareness (the third-order awareness) is reached in humans with the use of symbols, language, and the formation of concepts. These steps imply use of information inherent in the individual and the external world.

In recent times, physicists including von Weizsäcker, Diaz-Nafria, Zimmermann, and Lloyd have been referring to this concept of inherent, potential information and actualized information as part of their discussions on theories of information.[6]

Matter, energy, information, space, and time are the fabrics of nature. Both energy and information interact with matter to cause a change in structure in space and in time. For example,

---

[5] Lloyd, S. 2017

[6] von Weizsäcker, C. F. 2006; Diaz-Nafria, J. and Zimmermann E. 2013; and Lloyd, S. 2007

milk becomes butter. Or a seed becomes a plant. Information inherent in the milk and the seed are potential for butter and the plant respectively. When appropriate amount of energy becomes available, this *potential information* becomes *actualized information* in the form of butter or a plant. Information inherent in the matter specifies the changes to be initiated in time.

Energy is quantifiable. So is information. We are also told that information, once created, cannot be destroyed. It can only be transferred.

Classical physics has been focused on matter and energy until now. Physicists have been discussing for several decades that information may be a third fundamental unit after matter and energy. Indeed, Lloyd[7] points out that the universe itself is a quantum computer and that every elementary particle can register and process information. Lloyd points out that energy and information are intertwined and that they play a complementary role.

All of us know that energy is needed to get any work done. But the system should know what to do. That is where information comes in. To quote Lloyd again: "To do anything requires energy. To specify what is done requires information." Both energy and information interact with matter. Information is a fundamental unit of nature inherent in matter to be acted on by energy.

So, what is the message?

This is the age of information technology. It has revolutionized the way we live and communicate. It has also created conditions in which truth and lies demand equal attention, lies and rumors spread faster than truth, and people

---

[7] Seth Lloyd

are sequestered into their own information "silos." Scientists and scholars point out that social media, as part of IT, has disrupted collective human behavior. This is because of inherent defects in human psychology, business models that run social media, and unwise use of IT and media.

At a spiritual level, information is part of consciousness both at an individual level and at a cosmic level. It is one of the connecting substrata. Reflecting on one's own consciousness can lead to connecting with other lives and with the cosmos.

2. There is no useless knowledge.

Here is the story of how cultural attitudes helped develop the US to become the world leader in all branches of science during the twentieth century and how these attitudes have changed over the past few years. The story begins in the late 1800s and into the early 1900s.

One of the early publications that emphasized the need for basic research was a monograph published in 1939 with the title *Usefulness of Useless Knowledge* by Abraham Flexner, a pioneer in education, particularly graduate education. Among his accomplishments, the two most dominant ones are the establishment of the Institute for Advanced Study in Princeton and the famous *Flexner Report*, which changed the way medicine is taught and practiced in the US today.

The Institute for Advanced Study attracted some of the best minds from here and abroad. The list includes Albert Einstein, J. Robert Oppenheimer, Hermann Weyl, John von Neumann, and Kurt Gödel. The *Flexner Report* summarized the state of medical education in the US in the early 1900s and suggested several changes, which laid the foundation for making medical education and research in the US the best in the world.

The Institute for Advanced Study became "a center for curiosity-driven basic research." Its mission statement says: "It is to assemble a group of scientists and scholars who with their pupils and assistants may devote themselves to the task of pushing beyond the present limits of human knowledge and to the training of those who may 'carry on' in this sense." This is the atmosphere that attracted the world's best intellectual talent. This is also the theme of Flexner's monograph on the *Usefulness of Useless Knowledge*.

This report and the Institute for Advanced Study were the stimuli for support for basic research in several universities in the US during the earlier part of the twentieth century. Basic research is systematic study of observable facts and phenomena performed without any specific practical applications in mind. Abraham Flexner pointed out that what appears to be pursuit of useless knowledge may be very important to develop useful knowledge and useful products.

This is different from applied science in which scientific studies are performed using available scientific knowledge to develop practical applications. This step is crucial for the development of technologies. Applied research also took off attracting talents from all over the world when the "Report to the President" from Vannever Bush came in 1947. The second half of the twentieth century was the glorious period of scientific developments in all fields.

Fundamental studies to understand how electricity works, what the building blocks of atoms are, how genetic messages are carried from one generation to the next, what the best methods for distant communication are, how the three-dimensional structure of molecules determine chemical interactions were conducted mainly out of curiosity—just to know. Such basic sciences were considered essential for advancing our knowledge of the universe and development of new technologies. Even at the peak of its glory, there were skeptics who did not understand scientists who were working in their "ivory towers" studying esoteric fields, pursuing the so-called "useless knowledge."

Many did not realize that these were the studies that made technological advances such as radio, television, mobile phones, GPS units, computers and all the medical advances possible. Many do not realize it even now. The current emphasis is on applied science, which, of course, is important. The current focus is not just "curiosity" but development of commercial products and increases in the share value of corporations that support research.

Monetary support moved away from support of basic research, where scientists followed knowledge for knowledge's sake, to applied science. The goal of science (and of scientists) also moved from understanding nature to "explain, predict, and control (nature)." Many new technologies evolved making human life healthier and "better." But these new technologies came also with their negative consequences.

After a century of explosion of scientific knowledge and development of incredible technologies, we are now facing the negative effects of unsustainable growth and unintended consequences of technologies. This has resulted in changes in cultural attitudes to science.

The current climate is one of anti-scientific sentiments driving collective human behavior such as public health precautions and educational policies. There are vaccine-deniers and climate-change deniers. Books are banned from public libraries. Specific topics are not to be taught in schools and colleges. Policy decisions are made not based on scientific evidence but on political beliefs.

So, what is the message?

We need both kinds of scientific research. One is based on curiosity to understand nature and its laws. It is not product driven. Products, if any, are byproducts. Very few scientists will be able to pursue knowledge for its own sake without support to make a living.

The other is technological research with a specific product in mind. This kind of research gets more support because of its earning potential.

3. Science and technology are not the problems. Our collective behavior is.

Science as pursuit of knowledge for the sake of knowledge and driven by curiosity is not in favor. Who wants "useless" knowledge that does not lead to application? Besides, there is no money in it. The focus is on applied science made possible by technology to produce consumable products. Unfortunately, every technology comes with its own problems.

As Abraham Flexner pointed out, scientists like Hertz and Maxwell, who did the basic research on electricity, did their work simply out of curiosity, to understand the world. They did not even know what their discoveries would lead to. The successes of science itself has brought on several problems due to the industries enabled by science. These industries and associated technologies are intended to make life easier for all. However, there are negative sides to all of them (such as industrial waste) and inevitable consequences that annoy us. For example, industrialization also led to urbanization, overcrowding, over-utilization of natural resources, and the current climate crisis.

Basic research on the chemistry of carbon was a good thing. But it also made dynamite possible! Basic research on atom was a good thing. But we have atom bomb as one of its real consequences. CRISP-R technology is a great advance. But it also made it possible for a Chinese physician to use this technology for unethical purpose. Claude Shannon's work on the basic science of information gave us digital technology. But it has created social media with all its beneficial and harmful ramifications. Now comes Artificial Intelligence (AI) with lots of fanfare. But we know for sure it will have unintended consequences just like any new technology does.

We do not like the unintended consequences of technology. But that dislike gets transferred to science in general. I believe that the current resistance to science relates to the unintended consequences of technologies based on science and not to the basic science itself. We conflate one with the other. As pointed out by Lord Reyleigh, past president of the Royal Society, "The disasters are due to the folly of man, not the intention of science."

The Gap between People and Science

This is also a time when the public has lost trust in all institutions, including governments, the judicial system, and health care.

Most people want simple solutions and "yes" or "no" answers. They do not want to hear complicated scientific explanations with nuances, which confuses them. But science and scientific methods lead to the closest approximation to truth based on available evidence. By the nature of scientific methods, conclusions are tentative until further evidence comes in to support or challenge.

Scientists do change their minds when new data that contradicts prior conclusions becomes available. They are supposed to. That is the strength of science. Here is a very simple recent example from pediatrics. For a long time, pediatricians advised mothers to put babies on their stomachs (belly) to sleep. Now they recommend that babies be put on their backs to sleep. It is not because they do not know or not sure. They have new facts they need to incorporate into the new recommendation. New data suggests that Sudden Death Syndrome is less common in babies who are placed to sleep on their backs.

But for most people, this sounds like evasion. They think that scientists themselves do not know and keep changing their minds. Vested interests use this as an opening to spread their anti-scientific messages and alternate theories.

Another interesting phenomenon in the current age is that knowledge is so vast and so compartmentalized that there is an expert for not only every branch of science and technology but also for every aspect of life. The result is that the common person, even an "educated" one, feels inadequate dealing with everyday aspects of life. People think they have to ask the so-called expert on anything, from what brand of soap to buy to how to toilet train their child. There are, of course, many self-proclaimed experts, each one giving a different advice. That leaves the common person feeling confused and alienated. As pointed out by Walker Percy, they feel like a castaway in an island looking for "a message in the bottle" with a solution.

Deceptive Science

Some organizations that support research cover up data that contradict their position. They promote data favorable to their organization or industry. But this happened because a few scientists working for the industries lowered their standards and let it happen for their own reasons. "Whistle blowers" were "let go." Some organizations knowingly and purposefully sow seeds of doubt in the minds of people (example: tobacco industry, climate change deniers). This has become easier in this era of social media, fake news, and AI.

A few scientists misuse their position for power, position, or monetary rewards as outlined in the Lysenko affair *(see below)*.

Scientific method demands empirical proof for acceptance. Older philosophical systems such as Epicurean in the West and Charavaka in the East demanded evidence as the only acceptable support for any belief. Unfortunately, some scientists take this extreme position and denigrate and reject subjective experiences and subjective data. This turns off many who tend to act based on faith and experience-based studies.

There is plenty of poorly conducted scientific research and pseudo-science masquerading as science. Until recently, scientific studies took several years to perform and document. When these studies were written and submitted to journals, they went through rigorous quality control by editors and reviewers. Two developments have corrupted this system. One is the conflict of interest of either the authors or the reviewers influencing the decision on publication. This has been addressed adequately by some journals, but not by all. The other reason is the publication of unverified data on the Internet and in social media without peer review and quality control. What havoc AI-generated articles will bring we do not know!

There is an additional problem of "revolving door" between science and the agencies that review their products (as in pharmaceutical industry). Although there could be some potential benefits to both the agencies and the industries, the "revolving door" also poses ethical and policy challenges undermining public trust.[8] The presence of former industry personnel on the review boards may influence regulatory decisions. It may also influence policy decisions in favor of the interest of the industry.

---

[8] Maghani and Kuzma, 2010

Communication and Science

News media perform a poor job of reporting scientific advances. They are looking for dramatic ideas for their "Breaking News" banner. They report scientific talks and publications without applying rigorous criteria, which misleads the public. In fact, news reporters need training in reporting scientific studies.

Scientists, in general, are not good and effective communicators. This is because the scientist, to be a good scientist, must take a posture of objectivity about the external world to discover the underlying principles and causes. A good scientist is seeking the truth. But the common person has his needs for daily life. They are based on his subjective perceptions, needs, and context. He is confused by the nuances, technical jargons, and multiple opinions from self-proclaimed experts.

There is a gap between scientists and the public. That gap must be bridged with effective communication. Scientists need training in making their studies accessible to the public and to counter the deluge of pseudo-science and "conspiracy theories" on the Internet and social media.

Politics and Science

Finally, politicians have started controlling what science can and cannot do and what teachers can and cannot teach in schools. Political control of science is a dangerous trend. We have forgotten that modern science started flourishing only after the control of science by outside influences stopped. We have also forgotten what happened to biological sciences in the former Soviet Union due to denial of science, encouragement of pseudo-science, and pushing "state-mandated" version of science.

This is recent history from Russia and explains why Russia, which is a powerhouse in mathematics and science, lags so far behind in medicine and biological sciences. This was also responsible for the great famine in Russia. This is famously known as "Lysenkoism."

A Case Study of Bad Science

The following summary of "Lysenkoism" is based on an article with the title "Lysenkoism Against Genetics."[9]

Trofim Lysenko, was an agronomist who became an important figure in the Soviet Union during the cold-war era under Stalin and dominated the direction of research in genetics for close to thirty years. During this time, genetics was labelled as "idealistic pseudo-biology and anti-national." Stalin demanded loyalty to communist ideology in science and was replacing academicians and intellectuals with workers from peasant families. Although Lysenko had no credibility as a scientist, he was an agronomist and was from a peasant family. With Stalin's support, he became the head of the Lenin All-Union Academy of Agricultural Sciences.

His research on the so-called "new agricultural techniques" was flawed, and the results did not confirm his claim of increased yield of winter crops. He used some ideas that had been developed earlier by a Russian plant breeder by name Ivan Michurin. Lysenko mixed some of his personal ideas with those of Michurin and called it Michurinism. This combined with the political control of genetics research and plant breeding came to be known as "Lysenkoism."

Scientists who questioned Lysenko's work and ideas were silenced or driven out of the country. Some even committed suicide when forced to follow his concepts and hypotheses.

---

[9] Borinskaya, Ermolaev, and Kolchinsky, 2019

Lysenko promised to end the post-war famine in Russia by increasing agricultural production using his idea called "vernalization," an idea which had already been discredited by research done in Russia, Germany, and the US. This idea was based on the premise that the seeds can be "trained" to become resistant to harsh frost. Lysenko and his follower Isai Prezent, head of the Society of Marxist Biologists, rejected the existence of genes and postulated that inheritance can be transformed via "retraining" of plants. Obviously, his methods did not work, resulting in famine not only in Russia but also in other Eastern bloc countries where Lysenkoism was the favored kind of genetics.

Lysenkoism continued for several more years and had profound effects setting back biological research in Russia. Lysenkoism affected education and research in biology for several generations of students. The consequences persist even today.

So, what is the message?

Scientific developments in the past few centuries have benefitted humanity immensely. Life span has improved. Infant mortality and maternal mortality have been brought down. Fewer people are living below poverty line. Most major infectious diseases have been controlled or eliminated. There are effective medicines for most major diseases. Even some forms of cancers can be cured. We can communicate with anyone anywhere in the world in an instant, and even "meet" in virtual space. We can land on the moon and send capsules carrying messages to interstellar space. All of these were made possible because of objective scientific approach to solving problems.

Yes, all the advances have come with costs. Life is way more complicated. Climate has become disastrous and unpredictable. Species are disappearing. Earth's resources, even sand and drinkable water are being depleted. Human wastes are choking rivers, landscapes, and the ocean.

But the answer to solving our current problems is not in rejecting science and scientific approach. The results can be equally if not more dangerous. Because of people refusing to get vaccinated against mumps and measles, we are already seeing resurgence of these diseases in some areas. As a physician who has seen the ravages caused by these diseases, I would not want to see future generations of children die of these diseases.

What is needed is a balanced approach to new technologies, not rejection of scientific thinking and approach to solving problems.

We should not accept new technologies until they have been tested reasonably well and the dangers are fully understood and prepared for. People with monetary interests will push new technologies to the market, prematurely. But you, my readers, will have to set up conditions and set up safeguards before the release of new technologies. AI-driven products are probably the best examples.

This can be done as was shown with the Human Genome Project. At the start of the Human Genome Project, a program to examine its ethical, legal, and social implications was developed. It was charged with identifying major issues of concern and develop policy recommendations and guidelines to ensure that genetic information is used appropriately. A similar effort is under way to protect humanity from the misuse of CRISP-R technology.

My wish is that you, the readers and shapers of the future, help set guidelines and guardrails whenever any new technology arrives.

4. Life is not matter but depends on matter. Life is more than biology.

Life must be understood from both a scientific point of view and a spiritual point of view. Science is needed with its tools for understanding the biology, chemistry, and physics of the human body and of all forms of life. Spirituality is needed to understand the mystery of life itself and of consciousness. Science can help understand the laws of nature and the "how" of life. But spirituality is needed to think about the "why" of life.

Why life? Why consciousness?

Now life and consciousness also are also coming under the scrutiny of science and scientific methods. When I entered the field of medicine, patients were declared dead when the heart stopped beating and there was no breathing. With the incredible advances in biology and medicine, breathing can be maintained artificially and a heart that had stopped can be started back. Now, there is something called "brain death," which is defined by recording electrical signals from the brain. We cannot define *life* in simple terms. We used to be able to define *death*. But not any more.

Consciousness was a prohibited area for research when I entered medicine almost seventy years back. Now it is a major topic for research. But which is primordial—Life or Mind (i.e., consciousness)?

In Book 1, Section 164 of the *Rg Veda*, known as *Asya Vaamasya Sukta*, Rishi Dirghatamas says:

> The mortal and the immortal came from the source. Amid immortal was the mortal, which had breath (prana), movement, and from which the mind came.

He refers to the combination of breath, movement, and thoughts, which distinguishes the animated mortal.

Therefore, my first question will be "What is life" before I ask, "Who am I?"

Body, Mind, and Life

The mind depends on life for its manifestation. Mind appears only in a body with life. Without life, the body is "dead meat." That is why "what is life?" needs reflection before asking "Who am I?"

What is life? Why life? How did it come about?

I do not know whether we can ever find the answer for the questions on the "why" and the "what" of life. But asking that question will give us humility and a better answer to the question "Who am I?" because this question is about all of life, all lives. Trying to pursue the question will make us more considerate and compassionate towards all life-forms.

Is "life" unique and peculiar only to this earth and this universe we know of, or is there life elsewhere? On this earth, why is it that over the eons, many billions and trillions of lives have come and gone? Why does Mother Nature "behave" as if life is not her primary interest or concern, since she creates and destroys them? She treats life as if all life forms including humans are dry leaves at the end of autumn to be cleaned up and burnt or buried! Maybe life is not so important in the big picture.

Thinking deeply about life in general, there are three basic undeniable evident characteristics:

1. Life is not matter. But it depends on matter. It is a state, a state of being. It can exist only in a body made of matter. It cannot exist in vacant space, unlike matter and particles and energy fields. How can life exist as a concept without a material body? There is no function for the mind without the body.
2. For life to be present, there must be an exchange of energy. It is the movement of energy between two bodies with various levels of energy. The basis of life is exchange of energy.
3. Three important, inherent characteristics of life seem to be: Self-protection and escaping danger, seeking dependable sources of energy, and reproduction of the species.

Let's look more deeply from the scientific point of view to see what life might be.

Life is a Process

What is life? From the biological point of view, there is no single agreed-upon definition of "life." However, we can describe what constitutes life. In other words, we can list life's universal properties, tendencies, and realities.

Life is a process and not a substance, as noted by Sean Carroll. Any definition of life should include a capacity for self-replication and a capacity for evolution, which means a capacity for genetic changes to meet new challenges. In short, "life is any self-replicating, evolving system." NASA adopted a working definition of living organism as "a self-sustaining chemical system capable of Darwinian evolution."

At a very basic level, life requires exchange of energy. In most terrestrial lifeforms, it manifests as breathing. Even in this breathing, there is difference between breathing of animals and breathing of plants. Life in water also requires energy exchange, but by a different mechanism. Is it any wonder that oriental systems emphasize control of breathing as an essential step in meditation? Ultimately, the source of energy for all forms of life on this planet is the Sun. Is it any wonder that all early traditions and religions worshiped the sun as a God?

Biological Properties of Life

Once a life-form comes into being, what are its inherent biological properties? Science is better equipped to answer this question. The following is an answer given by Daniel Koshland, a distinguished scientist, who used to be the editor of *Science,* a magazine published by the American Association for the Advancement of Science (AAAS).

He identified seven common thermodynamic and kinetic factors by which life and living systems operate. He gave them an acronym "PICERAS" and called them the "Seven Pillars of Life." They are:

1. Program: organized plan describing both the ingredients and the kinetics of interaction between the ingredients.
2. Improvisation: allowing the programs to change if and when the environment changes.
3. Compartmentalization: providing special containers in which concentrations of essential chemical ingredients can be maintained in an ideal state and protected from the outside.

4. Energy: availability of continuous source of energy and ability to exchange energy in an open system.
5. Regeneration: includes regeneration of essential constituents and reproduction.
6. Adaptability: different from improvisation in that this is a behavioral response from within the existing repertoire and not a change in the fundamental program itself.
7. Seclusion: of pathways that "allows thousands of reactions to occur with high efficiency in the tiny volume of a cell, while simultaneously receiving selective signals that ensure an appropriate response to environmental changes."

Tendencies of Life

What are the inherent tendencies of life?

Life just wants to be and wants to live forever. Have we not heard the words "clinging to life?" Bill Bryson summarized it best in his book, *A Short History of Nearly Everything*, as follows:

> Life wants to be; life does not want to be much; life from time to time goes extinct. To this we may add a fourth: life goes on.

The other inherent tendency of life is a built-in need—an urge to reproduce. We would not be here but for this urge. We need not overemphasize it. And there is no use denying it either. It is part of life.

This is a realistic summary of life from a biological point of view.

Realities of Life

What are the inherent realities of life?

We all know that life is impermanent. Death is inevitable. That is the reality. In an eloquent passage, Bill Bryson points out how we are made of trillions of atoms assembled mysteriously to create me and you. These atoms came out of this earth and ultimately from the sun and the stars. We are indeed made of stardust. But these atoms which came together to make you and me are "mindless particles," "not alive themselves." Then, for reasons which are not known to us, these atoms "silently disassemble, shut you and me down and go off to do other things."[10]

Another reality of human life is loneliness. Life is a lonely struggle, particularly at moments of disease and stress. Death is a personal experience and a lonely journey. No one can take our burden, feel our pain, or die for us.

Reality of Death

Here is the central conflict. The life wants to live forever. But it is impermanent. How can we deal with this conflict? There are only a limited number of ways we can deal with the reality of death:

> We can put up a fight, in vain.
> We can accept it gracefully.
> We can accept it grudgingly.
> We can deny and pretend we are immortal.
> We can build imaginary future abodes.
> We can practice rituals to avoid it.

Various cultures have tried all these avenues and more. My preference is to accept the reality of death gracefully and live this one life following some virtues (called *dharma*) appropriate

---

[10] Bryson, 2004

to my stage in life. I can be prudent and considerate in my actions. I can be aware of the interconnectedness of our lives without losing the identity of my personal self. I can be detached without getting disengaged.

I can develop an inner compass to connect with and relate to this universe and an inner policeman to direct me in this world. I can practice compassion and universal love. I can be humble.

So, what is the message?

"I" am just a part of that whole called "life." The concepts of "I" and "mine" came later and separated me from others and the whole. By reflecting universality and fullness of life, we can develop respect, love, and compassion for all lives. Hopefully, our selfish view of life will retreat to the background and let us see the mystery and uniqueness of life itself.

5. Time is eternal and ever-changing.

I am not a physicist or a philosopher. But that did not stop me from wondering about the origins of the physical universe and the concept of time.

Here is a thought-experiment. I imagine myself on the banks of a river at the foothills of the Himalayas 4,000 years back, standing next to Rishi Prajapati, moved by the majesty of the snow-covered peaks, listening to the eerie silence around me, broken only by the sounds of the water and the voices of the birds. I wonder how all of this came about. What was there before? Was there something or nothing? How can something come out of nothing? Was earth there? Or the sky? Was it all darkness? When did the first ray of light come? Who knows and can explain how the manifest came out of the unmanifest?

These are not just my imagination. This is my translation of the original mystic poem attributed to Rishi Prajapati from the *Rg Veda* compiled almost 4,000 years back.

Around the same time, another visionary by the name of Rishi Dirghatamas asks, in the *Asya Vaamasya Sukta*:

> I, who am young, simple, and ignorant with undiscerning mind ask thee the whereabouts of those who are referred to as *devas* (deities)…
>
> I do not know who or what I am, yet I am wandering around tied to this mystery. …

> I, the ignorant, ask the sages who know. Since I do not know, I ask for the sake of acquiring knowledge. Please tell me. Who is that mysterious unborn who has established these six regions?

What humility! How true those sentiments are! Rishi Dirghatamas concludes by saying:

> They call that Divine Mystery as Indra, Mitra, Varuna, and Agni. The sages speak of the One by many names.

When I think about the universe and the mystery of its origin, I have to think about space and time.

Space is immeasurable. If it is limited, limited by what? If the Big Bang theory is correct, what did the expanding universe expand into?

Is time eternal and linear or is it eternal and cyclic? If time is not eternal, when did it start? What was there before that?

What is Time?

Let me start my answer with another thought experiment.

Suppose there is a planet in the Andromeda Galaxy, and it supports intelligent life. Suppose that one of those life-units (it may not resemble humans at all; but a human is all our imagination can conjure up) just invented a machine that can "see" deep into space. Suppose that life-unit (let us call that "man," by a name: LU) stumbles upon earth while looking through the scope. What will that LU see?

Since the distance between our galaxy and the Andromeda galaxy is two million light years, the image LU sees must be two million years old! That means LU is not seeing the present world. That will take two million more years to happen.

The first fact then is the lack of concordance of time. There is no simultaneity. LU's present is my past. My present is LU's future. In fact, even within short distance, your time is different from mine. By the time I type these words, my thoughts that initiated these words are a few seconds old. The sun we see is eight minutes old!

If what LU sees is two million years old, will the LU be seeing a world full of Neanderthals? Using the same logic, if LU were in a galaxy five billion light years away, will the LU not see the world at all since it had not come into existence!

That is spooky enough. Imagine LU's machine able to generate details like the images we get from the GPS or from the Hubble Telescope. If so, LU must be able see the Neanderthals. Why not? We can see tiny pebbles from the surface of the moon and Mars. LU is receiving image signals from two million light years away. But the puzzle is that the Neanderthals died millions of years ago. We, living in this world, cannot see them "now." But LU can see them.

It is possible because the photons generated two million years back are still traveling in space. Why not? We see through Hubble Telescope events that occurred millions of light-years back. We are still receiving radio signals from events from the early moments of the "big bang," which occurred billions of years back.

There are photon signals from several TV stations all around us. There are radio signals from several AM and FM stations all around us. I just need a device to capture those waves for me to see them or hear them. Those images from two million years must be there in space. Those images should, at the least, carry the gross image of the world as it was two million years back, if not the details of every life form on earth. That is the spookier part.

Am I saying that even after the Neanderthals have died, their "form" is still floating in space in the form of photons for an indefinite period? Yes, that is my conjecture. However, those forms are not real. They are only in a potential wave form. They cannot be actualized into "perceptible" form unless there is an observer at a distance! If there is no observer with an instrument, there will be an "appearance" of "nothing" or a void.

Why do I foolishly enter an arena that even the minds of Albert Einstein and Stephen Hawking could not decipher? I certainly do not have knowledge of physics or astronomy. But I experience time, all the time, and think about it often. Why should I not reflect on time using common sense and intuition?

Time is a Concept

My intuition tells me that time is phenomenal, a concept to comprehend movements and physical changes. Time might have been present before "life" came on the scene. But there was no one to call it "time." Life is a mystery. Time is a greater mystery.

Once humans came into the scene and found the ability to speak and name things, the word "time" was invented to explain changes that take place in front of their eyes, such as birth and death, sun rising and setting, moon growing and diminishing, trees blooming year after year. The concept of time was also needed to explain the relationship between objects during movement, since movement implies space, and time to traverse the space.

Time is a constant of the universe, but only as the present moment. For the rest of the "time," it is impermanent, comes as the future, and recedes away as the past.

Time has two parts to our perception. So suggests the Tamil poet, Kannadasan. Time is like a two-wheeled cart. One wheel stays fresh. The other decays and reforms, ever-changing. It is only in reference to the ever-fresh *eternal* time that we perceive the *ever-changing* time.

Plants and animals perceive time too, but in another sense. If it is not so, how can leaves change color at the approach of winter? How do birds start building nests long before they lay their eggs? All the plants and animals have built-in genes that cycle their metabolism to be in rhythm with sunlight.

Time implies space and change. Does time cause change or do changes induce perception of time? Why do changes occur? If things were static without change, would there be time?

What was there before time? What a silly question. Is it? Do we not imply that there was a beginning when we say time? If so, how can time be there without beginning? If it had a beginning, what was there before? If there was a "before," when and how did it start? Why?

Time is infinite and stationary, like a stretched string. Or maybe like a membrane stretched into a massive round or elliptical ball reflecting the shape of the movements of the planets, stars, and constellations. We move along the string, from birth to death through series of changes, and think time is passing. But we are the ones passing or moving along the fixed dimension of "time."

In other words, time is eternal. Time as experienced by a living organism is based on its perception of movement and changes (such as appearances and disappearances). The movement of the earth around the sun, and the consequent day and night cycle, was probably the first human observation of what we now call time. If we were to enter deep space, there would be only darkness. What is time in such deep darkness with no cycles of darkness and light, except for the concept of time we humans carry with us based on existence in this world of cyclic periods of light and darkness?

Time is not an illusion, however. It is a mirage, neither real nor unreal. It is both, depending on the point of view. Since any movement in space implies "passage of time," time exists in the background as an eternal, non-moving phenomenon. In that sense it is a fixed entity. But it requires a human (or some such entity) with the ability to perceive changes and movement to conceptualize it and give it a name. Thus, time becomes phenomenal and real for us.

How We Experience Time

In the vast space of the universe, when something like a planet moves, it will keep moving as long as there is no impediment. This will be true at the atomic level too. That unimpeded movement gives a sense of time for a sentient being like human. This is linear time.

If light and dark appear alternately, that will also give a sense of cyclic time. If during cyclic times of days and nights, new "things" appear and disappear or undergo changes, we experience cyclic time. In addition, our mind as it is constituted looks for causes and results. It also looks for beginning and end reinforcing the idea of linear phenomenal time.

Will we experience time if there are no light-and-dark cycles? Will we experience time if there are no changes in animals, plants, mountains, oceans, and rivers? If changes occur in the mountains and oceans as they have been for millennia, and there is no one to perceive them, will there be a concept of time?

Put it differently, space is real whether a sentient being is there or not. But time is not. It is a concept or a construct to explain movement and changes, for a sentient being, when there is one.

So, what is the message?

Time is both real and phenomenal. There are only three ways we can deal with Time. As individuals and collectively, we can live in the past, live in the present, or in the future.

PART II. SPIRITUALITY

When one of my grandchildren asked what I mean by "spirituality," I could not answer with a simple definition.

Spirituality is acknowledging that life is special and sacred. If it is special and sacred for me, it is special and sacred for you, and it is special and sacred for every form of life. Therefore, acknowledging the common sacredness and dignity of all forms of life and acting with respect and compassion is spirituality.

Spirituality is an attitude of the mind to explore the cosmos and nature. It is based on personal reflection on the big philosophical questions with an open mind, humility, and compassion. It is an attitude of mind and way of deep reflection leading to insights about our own values and our purpose in life. Practice of spirituality should lead to tolerance to other's point of view, inner peace, and harmony with the outer world.

Roots of My Spirituality

My thoughts on spirituality are based both on my upbringing in India and my life in the US amongst people of different faiths in both countries. I was influenced by my own journey into Hinduism and Buddhism by reading some of the original texts, experiences in a week-long retreat with Rev. Thich Nhat Hanh on two occasions, and several decades of daily meditation. I have also read the Bible in different versions and writings of Thomas Kempis, St. Augustine, Plotinus, and others. I have read some translations of the Qur'an and of the Talmud.

However, my organization of this knowledge into a personal view came out of synthesizing them based on my understanding of the cultures, traditions, faiths, sacred texts, and myths from the point of view of a cultural anthropologist and objectivity of scientific method. I tried to understand how each of these cultures and religions answered the fundamental questions listed at the beginning of this book, such as "What is life?", "What is the cosmos?", "Who am I?" and "What is my relationship to others and to this cosmos?"

I was born and raised in an orthodox Hindu family. Our family emphasized rituals and expected strict adherence but did not explain the reasons or symbolism behind them. I learnt all the rituals and prayers but without knowing the meaning. Fortunately, I had a working knowledge of Sanskrit and therefore started reading some of the foundational texts such as *Bhagavad Gita* during my days in medical school.

After coming to the United States, my curiosity to learn more about my roots increased. In addition, I found myself having to explain my tradition to my colleagues and friends. They were curious and interested. Therefore, I started reading more. Two of the earliest books I read were Aldous Huxley's *Perennial Philosophy* and Swami Atmananda's book, *Sankara's Teachings in His Own Words.* I was completely captivated by Sankara's (Adi Sankara, as I refer to him) brilliance, open mind, and explanations. His comments led me to the *Brahma Sutra* and a few of the *Upanishads.*

Later, when my children were growing up, they started asking questions about Indian (Hindu) customs, festivals, and ways of worship. They wanted to know "why" we do things the way we do. I had to find out since I too believed in the meaning behind things more than in the symbols. I started reading with special focus on explanations on how several schools of thought started in India and on the meaning of rituals. After retirement, there was more time. With the arrival of the internet, I was able to access the classic texts online. I started reading classic texts such as *Rg Veda*, Patanjali's *Yoga Sastra* and the *Mahabharata*.

One other major event expanded my field of spiritual thinking even more. That happened when I was visiting Indonesia and was introduced to a book on Buddha with the title *Old Path, New Clouds* by Rev. Thich Nhat Hahn. I liked the emphasis in Buddhism on living this life well and on compassion.

I decided to attend a week-long retreat with Rev. Thich Nhat Hanh when I learnt about mindfulness and various kinds of meditation. I was so impressed and my progress in spirituality improved so much after the first retreat, I attended a second one with Rev. Thich Nhat Hahn. I was impressed with the way Buddhist monks have developed practical methods for meditation anchored to the here and the now yet also make connections to the rest of the world and to the cosmos. In addition, I found that research in neurosciences lend empirical support to the meditation methods developed by Buddhist monks over several centuries.

Through my personal experience, I came to understand that spirituality is one component of all religions. But religions place more emphasis on other aspects such as rituals, prayers, sacred texts, sacred symbols, and beliefs. Religion is a group activity. Spirituality is activity of an individual, a personal search for meaning and connections to the universe. Therefore, it requires discipline and sustained personal effort. Spirituality is a personal activity which may or may not be part of any religion. One can practice spirituality without belief in any of the religions.

There is no clash between spirituality and science, but there is between religion, which emphasizes faith and obedience, and reason, which emphasizes questioning and verification.

One other thought about science in relation to spirituality. In this age of science and technology, the emphasis is on objective, analytic way of knowing. But scientific knowledge is only one way of knowing. To know about something objectively and "as it actually is", one has to know it through one's mind, heart and the spirit. It can help to look at the big cosmic picture, to look at our planet and also to consider other people and other lives with compassion.

Is it possible to weave strands of ideas from religion, spirituality, philosophy, and science and make a practical quilt? The following passages are my attempts at this task.

6. Myths are not statements of truth.

Growing up in a small town in India at a time when there were no streetlights, the night sky used to be dazzling. The moonlight was intense, particularly since the town is close to the equator. The stars were bright, and my grandmother used to tell approximate time at nights just by looking at the night sky. I am sad that there is so much light pollution, and you are growing up not having had a clear view of even the Milky Way.

Looking up at the night sky, I did wonder how the moon and the stars stayed up there without falling on our heads. I wondered how they came about. I still do. They are perennial mysteries.

Mysteries exist to be admired and not to be analyzed. Yet we keep asking, "How did this cosmos come about?", "How did life start?", "How did plants, animals and human came into being?", "Where did the first man and woman come from?" and so forth.

Creation Stories

Creation stories are based on the efforts of our ancestors to symbolize their imaginations and intuitions about the origins of this universe, the sun and the stars, the plants, animals, and humans. Creation stories are metaphors, although some of the stories may be based on actual historic events etched in the memories of those who lived at that time and passed on as stories—for example, the Great Floods, so common to most mythologies.

Myths are not meant to be interpreted literally. They must be valued for their importance to the transmission of traditions and values.

Myths are not for analysis and resolution. They are meant to inspire, to connect us to our own inner selves, to other lives and to the Cosmos. In this sense, myths are to spirituality what prayers are to devotion.

The remainder of this essay summarizes creation stories from various traditions. I encourage you to read them and ask yourself what they tell you about the culture they came from, and how they might influence your own understanding of life and the cosmos. Do you find them helpful? Do they conflict with each other? Use this chapter for your own expansion of knowledge and wonder.

Indian Creation Story

The Rg Veda, one of the earliest scriptures of Hinduism says that the "real" or the "First Thing" (*sat*) must have come from *asat* (no thing) because "in the beginning there was nothing." How can something come out of nothing? But *asat* does not mean non-existent. *Asat* must have meant "unmanifested" (*avyakta* in Sanskrit).

In Indian creation mythology, the progenitor of humanity is called Prajapati. "How did he come about?" is the first question. There was unmanifest energy of vital breath (*prana*) from which seven rishis came, says the scriptures. Rishis, who were neither God nor human, were the first creations. But they could not procreate themselves because they were "mental." Therefore, they combined themselves into a single body, a person, called Purusha. Two rishis formed the parts above the navel: two below the navel. One formed the right and another one made the left. One formed the base. There was no head. The rishis extracted all their indivicual energies, put them into a pot (*kalasam*) and that became the head. Now, there was a full person, Prajapati. But we know that Prajapati was also the creator. The usual chicken or egg dilemma.

But Prajapati is not *the* creator. He is just the *process* of creation. In one version, when he looked outward, a female appeared. That was Vac, which stards for word or speech. Vac was, in a way, his daughter. Prajapati united with Vac mentally and since nothing is external to h_m, it was he who became pregnant.

* * * *

Here is another version: In creating the universe, Prajapati wanted to create firm ground on which creatures can flourish. He created earth, sky, and heaven. Subsequently, the deities of the earth (*prithvi*), sky (*antariksha*), and celestial realm (*dhyau*) were born.

When he started doing penance with his arms raised, stars came out of the vault of his armpit. "He held his arms in darkness." After a thousand years, the wind (*vayu*) arose. Fire (*agni*) came from his mouth and asked for something to eat, an oblation. Terror struck Prajapati and his greatness escaped from his mouth in the form of *Vac*, speech. Vac is sound which dwells in space. The sound produced was his own.

* * * *

In another version, Prajapati did not want to be alone. He wanted company. He "created" Ushas, a female. When he wanted to co-habit with her, she got scared and ran away. She became a mare; Prajapati became a mare; they paired. She became a cow, and Prajapati became a bull and so on. That is how all the animals, birds, fish, and human came into being.

There are similar creation myths in every culture. The question is always how the first human came into being, and how did one become many. Here are some examples.

Bible

What is the creation myth in the Bible? In one version of the Bible (New International Version), the creation story is given Genesis 1 to 31.[11] It gives details of how God created heavens, earth, light, all the elements, all vegetation, planets, animals of the air and sea, and humans, giving humans dominion over all creation, all in six days. Genesis 2 then concludes the creation story by saying God blessed the seventh day as a day of rest.

Maori of New Zealand

According to the Maori myth, there was Te Kore (which stands for Nothing) in the beginning. Just silence. Nothing lasted for a long time. Then there was Te Po, the Long Night, dark and silent, which lasted for a long time. There was nothing to see and nothing to hear—just darkness and silence. From the Dark and the Silence emerged Papa Tu Anku or mother earth and Rangi Nui, father sky. They loved each other and embraced each other so close there was no space between them. There were many off-springs but none of them could escape the darkness. They were trapped between Tu Anku and Rangi Nui.

The children decided that they must separate their parents and start living. Tane, a son who was to become god of the forests, placed his feet on this father and slowly pushed him out. The parents were separated. Tane took some earth and made a woman, Hine Ahu One, the earth-formed maiden. She

---

[11] https://www.biblestudytools.com/genesis/1.html

gave birth to Hine Titama, a Dawn maiden. The children of Hine Titama and Tane became the men and women of the world.

Nordic Creation story

The Nordic creation myth also contains elements of void, chaos, and many coming from dismembering parts of one body (akin to the story of Prajapati). Initially, there was nothing except a deep, dark silent chasm called Ginnungagap between the lands of fire and ice. The heat and the cold of these worlds met at Ginnungagap. When the ice melted, drops of water made themselves into a giant called Ymir. The name Ymir means "a screamer." When Ymir slept, many giants came out of his sweat and his armpits.

As the ice melted, a cow by name Audhumla emerged. She fed on the salt licks and nourished Ymir with her milk. Her licks uncovered Buri (which means progenitor), who had a son named Bor. Bor had three sons by Bestla, the daughter of a giant named Bolthorn. The first of these sons was Odin who became the chief of the Aesir gods.

Odin and his brothers killed Ymir and fashioned the world from different parts of his body. The ocean came from his blood, the earth and soil from his skin and muscles, plants from his hair, cloud from his brains, and the sky from his skulls. Later, the gods made a man and a woman from the trunks of two trees, Aska and Embla.

Egypt

In the southern old kingdom of Egypt, it is said that initially there was nothing but dark water in which eight gods of power lived. They were like frogs and snakes and contained within themselves water, floods, darkness, and energy. After a long time, their energy broke through the water and *benben,* the primal mound, rose out of water. Thoth, the Ibis god, flew in with the cosmic egg and laid it on benben, the mound. Atum, the sun god, was born from this cosmic egg and contained the life force for all living beings and the potentiality for all non-living matter. He created his spouse from himself and all the gods and human. This myth also resembles the myth of golden egg in the Indian creation myths.

Native American

There are hundreds of Native American tribes with several different creation stories. However, the themes are common. First, these tribes do not have a word to describe "religion." There are no dogmas or scriptures either. In other words, there is no organized religion. The emphasis is on the harmony of life between plants, animals, and humans on this earth; the sanctity of earth; and respect for ancestral spirits. World existed from time immemorial, and man came later, after the plants and animals. The plants, animals, and birds know more about the earth than we do. We are here to take care of the earth we live in; not to trample upon it and just use it.

In his sensitive, firsthand experience, Charles Alexander Eastman (his Indian given name was Ohiyesa) writes in his book on *The Soul of the Indian* as follows:

> The elements and majestic forces in nature, Lightning, Wind, Water, Fire and Frost, were regarded with awe as spiritual powers, but always secondary and intermediate in character. We believed that the spirit pervades all creation and that every creature possesses a soul in some degree, though not necessarily a soul conscious of itself. The tree, the waterfall, the grizzly bear, each is an embodied Force, and as such an object of reverence.

There is a Great Spirit from which everything came, which blew its breath into all living creatures. There are references to sacred hills (Turtle Hill, Black Hill), World Tree (in the Sundance ceremony), and floods akin to these elements in other mythologies.

Two ideas struck me as very similar to the Vedic thoughts. One is from the Lakota tribe, who have the word combination *wa-ka,* which means "That which is That it is." It is literally the same as "Thou art That" or *tatvam asi.* The word *ka* also has a meaning like Brahman.

The other is the Hopi story about four worlds before the current one. It sounds very much like the four *yugas* (epochs) of the Indian mythology with increasing breaking down of virtues in succeeding worlds.

One other creation story from the natives of the Plains, such as Sioux, calls the first human as "The Man Who Was The First Created" (same idea as Prajapati). He had one younger brother who was killed by a "monster of the deep." To revive him, the First Man dug two holes at the banks of Great Water. He filled one with the bones of his brother. In the other he placed four stones and fire and chanted. He then sprinkled water on the heated stones. With the steam, "life appeared." When the First Man sprinkled water a second time the bones rattled. When he sprinkled water third time, there was some sound coming from the hole. When he sprinkled water the fourth time, he heard his brother's voice saying: "Let me out, brother." Thus came the first man on this earth from under the ground.

In this myth, the stone is sacred and revered. It is called Tunkan and represents grandfather. Number four stands for the four winds, four directions and the foursome of water, wind, fire, and other elements.

Intuit (Eskimo)

In the Inuit (Eskimo) tradition, Raven is the primordial life. Raven is a trickster or one who behaves against the customs of the society.

The Raven made this world and its waters by beating his wings. He had the powers of a man and a bird and can switch from one to the other by simply dipping his face in the water and taking it out. In the beginning, the earth was dark and silent. The Raven made mountains and fields and created pea-pod plants over the land. On the fifth day, a man came out of one of the pea-pods. The Raven was surprised that such a creature can come out of the plant he had created. The man was dizzy and confused and drank water from a pool. The Raven was flying above and observing the man. Neither was talking.

The Raven asked the man: "Who are you? Where did you come from?" The man said that he came out of the pea-pod. The Raven was surprised. He asked the man whether he had eaten, and the man said, "No." The Raven flew away and came back after four days with two raspberries and two heath berries. The man devoured them in one gulp. The Raven realized that the berries were not enough and so he created two sheep out of clay and waved his wings over them. The sheep came alive. The man had more food now.

The Raven created more sheep and let them graze far away so the man would not eat them all at once. Soon more men came out of the pea-pods. The Raven made fish, birds, and other animals and placed them away from these men, so they did not kill them all. The Raven also created a huge bear to make sure that men knew fear.

After a few days, the Raven noticed that the man was lonely. Therefore, he went to a place where the man could not see and created a clay figure and waved his wings over it. Out came a beautiful, soft creature. The Raven took her to the man and said: "This is woman, your helper and companion." Man was pleased and together they filled the earth with their children.

Common Themes in Creation Stories

A review of these creation myths shows that the common questions they address are: 1. After the first human being came, how did the others come? 2. Even if the first pair of male and female begot children by incest, where did the children get their spouses?

Common themes in the creation myths are a void and darkness or chaos in the beginning; water, tree, bird, or a snake in the creation story; the word as a powerful force; and many come from one by dismemberment of the first-born or splitting of the first one or by incest.

7. Who am I? How did I come about?

Science and spirituality are points of view, systems of philosophy. Both try to understand life and the cosmos. Science focuses on reproducible evidence and therefore is trustworthy as a basis for future actions. It breaks down the whole into parts to understand better. Spirituality is intuitive and understands the whole and nature as is.

I tend to synthesize science and spirituality whenever possible. I hope I am not going too far with the following thoughts.

When I read that the migration of birds depends on quantum changes in the molecules in their brains, something clicked. I remembered a short story with the title *Game Without End*. In this story, Italo Calvino spins his imagination into a game he plays with his friends when the early universe was making new atoms and galaxies were forming. In this game, each boy rolls one atom out of his collection of hydrogen atoms along the space curve. The kid whose atom went the farthest becomes the winner. The rule of the game says that when each one rolls the next set of atoms, he can touch his own atom and push it farther. But he can also push someone else's atom out of the way. He cautions to just roll the atom and "not to push too hard because when two hydrogen atoms knock together, Click! A deuterium atom might be formed" and hydrogen is no longer hydrogen.

Going back to atoms and molecules in the brain of migrating birds, it appears that quantum effects of earth's magnetism act on two specific molecules, Trp and FAD, in the brains of birds. Earth's magnetic force trips one electron to flip from one molecule to the other and triggers the release of neurotransmitters. This is coded as memory, which, in addition to other clues, helps the birds navigate. This is electromagnetic memory that depends on quantum particles.

If that is true for birds, mammals, and humans—and that is a big "if"—does it apply to the philosophical question of "Who am I"? My "I" is different from the one born many decades back in another part of the world. Every particle in this body has been replaced over the years—even the genetic material. How is it then that I am still me?

The fundamental particles that make me have changed. My location has changed. Many decades have passed. In other words, matter and energy keeping "me" together in space and time have changed. Yet I am still the same "I." How is that?

That is because the template is the same...like the famous philosophical experiment about an old chariot or a ship whose parts have all been replaced. Is it still the same chariot or ship? The parts are different. But the template is the same. It is another way of saying that the "form" is determined by information in the DNA, which gives us a stable but time-limited template.

The particles of the chemicals making up my current genes are different from the originals with which I was born. But the message has been kept the same by the genetic codes, which are molecules of information. Therefore my "form" is the same except for the changes in it due to passage of time. Information for the physical structure is the same.

The other common factor is my consciousness with its important function of memory. As pointed out by Buddha many centuries back, confirmed more recently by the work of Antonio Tomasio and others, "I" am made up of memories of events in my life (autobiographical memory) and a sense of ownership of those memories as mine (thanks to our insular cortex and anterior cingulate gyrus, etc.,). Therefore, I am aware and can say: "I am the continuity of what I was born with, although I look and think different." Others looking at me see that continuity too, giving me another point of reference.

Our ancestors were correct when they challenged us to think "Who am I?" Since particles are parts of matter that change over space and time, and since information, memory, and consciousness are subjects for scientific inquiry, it is a good time to reflect on this fundamental question.

Maybe Buddha was correct when he talked about "dependent co-arising" (*pratitya samutpada*) and said that "I am made of non-I elements."

If so, who am I?

I am part of, no —I am one with—the universe.

I am alive in this universe.

I am aware because I am alive.

Because I am aware, I am aware that I am alive.

Because I am aware, I am aware of the universe in which I am.

I am aware of me as part of the universe.

I can connect with all other lives with similar awareness.

I am the subject and the object of my awareness.

I am the subject of the object I am aware of.

I am the subject of the subject of the thought…

8. *"It shines; and it makes things shine."*[12]

9. *"Through what should one know the Knower?"*[13]

During the recent *Deepavali* (*Diwali*) celebration, I explained the meaning of lighting a lamp to my non-Hindu friends. This festival is special for the Hindu, Buddhist, Jain, and Sikh religions. Lighting a lamp is central to all other major religions too, for example, Hanukkah in the Jewish tradition, Christmas lights in the Christian tradition, the Sacred Fire as light at the Zoroastrian temple, and lighting of candles as part of Kwanzaa in several African traditions.

Light symbolizes spiritual awakening, removal of ignorance, and connections to the Divine presence. Aphorism 8 as given above is from a prayer during daily worship in Hinduism: *"tameva bantam anubhati sarvam; tasya bhasa sarvamidam vibhati."*[14] These words in Sanskrit suggest that the illuminating or self-revealing Light, which shines by itself, makes other things visible.

In this respect, consciousness is compared to light in Indian philosophy. Just as light does, consciousness makes other things known just by its presence. This is the basis of

---

12 *Mundaka Upanishad* 2:2:10

13 Yagnavalkya in *Brihadaranyaka Upanishad* 2:4:14

14 *Mundaka Upanishad* 2:2:10

meditation techniques that focus on the ultimate awareness, ultimate consciousness, the subject, by letting go of the objects of consciousness. That subject cannot be known. If it can be known, it becomes an object of knowledge. That subject can only be experienced in deep meditation.

How do we know the existence of light? By the absence of darkness. How do we know of the absence of darkness? By the appearance of objects to our senses. The light reflects off the objects and strikes our retina. The object was there already. Light made it visible. That is why the *Mundaka Upanishad* says: "It shines; and it makes things shine." This faculty may be attributed to the sun, any light and to Consciousness.

Light shows objects and in the process shows itself. So does our consciousness. It makes things known as both an object and as the subject of that experience of the object. It removes ignorance and brings knowledge. It is aware of light and darkness. That is the reason light and consciousness are special in the Vedic writings.

But does light always illuminate?

Having gotten up early in the morning, I was standing in my balcony and looking up at the beautiful sky. It was before sunrise and there was this partial moon, and I could see Venus and Jupiter also. A little later, as expected, these three celestial objects could not be seen. That made me think about the contradiction in the commonly stated philosophy that light removes darkness and illuminates everything.

Light does remove darkness, illuminates, and makes things known. (*tameva bhantam anubhati sarvam; tasya bhasa sarvamidam vibhati* says *Kathopanishad* 2:2:15) But does it? My observation this morning, which everyone else also has experienced, points to something else. Light can also hide things. Or at least it can make us blind to things that do exist.

Those planets and the stars are still hanging in space even during the day!

In a way, darkness IS, because light is. They "inter-are." Light can illuminate as well as hide. Knowledge can uncover as well as it can cover or confuse. Knowledge can be a hindrance to further knowledge if the mind is not curious and open. That is why we need the mind of a child, a beginner's mind, an innocent mind to see things as they truly are. Is that not what Buddha said?

10. "*My blood is red; so is yours. My tears are salty; so are yours.*" (*Buddha*)

Indian Vedic texts say that every human being on this planet is our family. Both Hindu and Buddhist meditations teach us to reflect on the fact that all of us are made of the same five elements (space, air, fire, water, and earth) of this universe and energized by the same force. That force, that animating force, called *Atman* (or *Brahman*) is in each one of us. *Ishopanishad* (6) says: "When one sees all beings in the Self (Atman) and one's Self in all beings there is no hatred in the heart."

When I reflected on this, I realized that our physical body is made with a neural structure (brain and nervous system) primarily to protect itself and survive. Therefore, we instinctively are self-centered and tend to compete. Because of this competition, we find the world full of winners and losers and the society marred by inequalities and injustices. "Freedom and Equality" do not go together too well, as noted by Will and Ariel Durant.[15]

That is because of inherent differences in our abilities and "accidents of birth." By "accident of birth," I mean that we are not born as male or female, speaking English or Spanish, in India or in Ireland by our choice. At birth, we are endowed with varying levels of intelligence and abilities. We arrive in this

---

[15] Will and Ariel Durant, 1968

world in a rich family or a poor family, in a metropolitan city or in Amazonian jungle, not by choice. Therefore, we tend to fall into different strata of the society.

We are bound to find ourselves in various positions of power and wealth. Physical and economic inequality are inevitable. Power and wealth tend to corrupt, which often operate to maintain social inequalities. The powerful will tend to exert their power since their mind is made to be selfish, just as it is in everyone else. Acceptance of equality in the sacredness of life itself, human dignity, and respect for every life is the antidote to such corruption.

Our neural organization is made not just for survival. It is also endowed with structures and chemicals associated with empathy, compassion, and socialization. Just as were born with certain inherent weaknesses, we were also born with certain inherent abilities and temperaments, strengths. We come as "a package." Given proper external conditions and internal tendencies, all potentialities can be developed in every individual. We can develop our strengths by looking deeply at our inner self and at the outer world with an open mind, understanding, and compassion. This is spirituality.

It is possible to learn to actuate our natural abilities to be compassionate and altruistic.

11. We can and must touch our "collective consciousness."

After reflecting on "Who am I" and "What is my relationship to the cosmos and to other lives on this planet," I wondered about our collective consciousness.

In defining "collective consciousness," I am defining consciousness in its generic meaning of awareness of ourselves and of the world around us. This is different from the sociological definition of Emile Durkheim, in which the term "collective consciousness" stands for common beliefs, values, and behavior within a society.

Is there an inborn collective consciousness, an awareness of one's own mind and of the minds of others?

Those were my thoughts when I was reading a pictorial essay on the "aerial acrobatics" of swarms of starlings. I have seen those swarms too (called *murmurations*). Obviously, each bird in the swarm knows the "mind and direction of movement" of its immediate neighbors, and all of them interconnect so that they have a "collective mind." Can it not be called a component of the collective consciousness of the starlings?

The same thought occurred to me when I was watching a group of birds flying alongside our boat for almost fifteen or twenty minutes when we were sailing between islands in the Galapagos. They were flying in formation with two birds in the lead position. Periodically, two birds would move from the end part of the formation and take over the front lead position.

How did they know that it was their turn to lead the pack and relieve the birds in the lead who have been using more energy than others and needed rest?

Several years back, I watched an osprey couple raise their brood on the banks of a river. It was amazing to see the male and the female taking turns watching the eggs. The female and the male will take turns bringing food for the chick. The female will teach the chick how to fly, and she will not leave the nest for good till the youngest one can take off on its own. How did the mother know it is her responsibility?

On another occasion while walking along a stream, I watched a duck floating along with three of her chicks. The mother was in front. When she approached a small fall in the gradient, creating a mini waterfall, the mother turned around and guided her chicks to the bank. She then led them by land to the water at the lower level. How did she know that it was not safe for her babies to approach the fall? What told her that it is her duty to protect them?

Is it not acceptable to call all this "collective consciousness" of the species—built in and inherent in their body, brain, mind, and psyche? We humans certainly have a collective consciousness if only we know how to touch it.

Part III. Society

In this section, I outline my thinking on how science, spirituality, and a cultural approach to fundamental facts of life shape the way of life in any society. My thoughts were greatly influenced by my early life during my formative years in India, and later by my work and family life in the United States. These ideas also grew out of travels to many countries and reading the writings of impactful authors from the countries I visited.

I grew up in a society whose history goes back to a pre-Christian era. My language is one of the classic languages of the world with a rich literature also going back to 2,000 years. I grew up in a small town of probably about 5,000 to 6,000 people. Given the caste and religious variations among the people, recognizable groups lived in separate but adjacent streets. For example, the brahmins lived in streets around the temple. Merchants lived in their section. Christians lived in another section of the town around a local church. Muslims lived in yet another section close to a mosque. But it appeared to me at that time, everyone accepted the status quo and there was harmony among the people.

Almost all families I knew lived in an extended family system. It was common to see three generations under one roof. The younger generation accepted the fact that it was their duty to care for the elders. Everyone in the street knew everyone else. It was not possible for someone to misbehave without the entire street knowing about it. Whenever there was happy occasion such as wedding or a sad event such as death, everyone around was there to help. The extended family system and the sharing and mutual support from the neighbors gave stability and benefited everybody.

Life was simple and needs were minimal. We did not even have electricity on our street until I was in middle school. We never had a phone in our house. There was poverty and many infectious diseases and none of the modern facilities. Yet, people were generally helpful and happy.

When I came to the US, the situation was totally different. At a personal level, I did not have any relatives here. I lived in an apartment that was part of the hospital in which I was training. I was responsible for taking care of my needs. There was no one to tell me what to do in my personal life. There was no one I could ask for help either.

But given the nature of the American society, the people were extremely friendly and helpful. I made friends with the physicians in town. They helped me get adjusted to this culture. Even some of the patients became friends and helped me understand American values, customs, and cultures. I realized that every culture develops its set of values and customs in relation to its geography and history and the contexts.

These thoughts were reinforced by my experiences with religion. There were no Hindu temples in the US at that time. Therefore, I went to churches and a few synagogues with some of my friends. When I was living in Chicago for one year, I used to go to the Bahai temple in Wilmette, Illinois, for meditation. My openness to other traditions and respect for them started at that time. Later, my curiosity helped me to learn more about other traditions.

My view of the society and of the universe was also influenced by the fact that I spent two years doing basic medical research with some brilliant medical scientists. I learnt the philosophy of science and the fundamentals of scientific methods. This was one of the dominant factors in shaping my world view of the societies in general. One of those scientific disciplines that fascinated me was cultural anthropology.

When I used a cultural anthropological perspective to understand the culture I grew up in and the culture in which I spent most of my life, my world view expanded. It became richer.

Cultural View of Science

Cultural attitudes have consequences. As mentioned earlier in the opening essay on science, five existential beliefs influence individual choices in every culture.[16] They define the culture's relationship to nature, relationship to human nature, relationship to time, view of human actions, and relationship to others. I pointed out earlier that Western cultures believe in controlling nature. That modal attitude is the force behind most of the advances in science.

Science tries to understand nature by breaking complex objects into parts and analyzing them. The knowledge obtained is an objective knowledge. Since it is an empirically derived knowledge based on objective facts, it is more reliable for certain purposes. When things, events and even personhood are analyzed as object, we know about that thing, event. But it is a manipulated knowledge, using words and logic—not a knowledge of the thing as is. As Prof. Nagle asked: "What is it like to be a bat?" He was referring to subjective and experiential knowledge, which science ignores.

In contrast, Eastern and Indigenous cultures consider that for knowledge to be complete, it must include knowledge of the object in all dimensions—physical, contextual, temporal,

---

16 Nolan Weil, 2017

and spiritual. Knowledge, to be complete, must be learned through the body, the "heart" (emotions), the mind (reason), and the spirit.

Cultural Attitudes to Commerce

Although commerce has been a crucial aspect of all cultures, mass production and consumerism are recent developments. Science and technology made mass production and mass consumption possible. A more recent development is the idea of commodification. A simple definition of the word commodification is turning something into a product that can be sold and bought. In the current climate goods, services and knowledge can be converted into a commodity available in the marketplace. Even medical care has been commodified. In the process of commodification, the monetary value of the product or service is the primary focus. The product or service is stripped of all other subjective and utilitarian values.

Commodification, commerce, and commercial enterprises have helped employ more people and get them out of poverty. That translates into improvement in health and quality of life for more people in the world. But factors related to commerce and industry, such as lack of ethics, have also contributed to significant social divides and inequalities. These inequalities were brought into clear focus during the recent pandemic.

The emphasis of large companies and corporations seems to be excessively tilted towards share values and profits. National priorities favoring the goals of big corporations seems to be on Gross National Product (GDP) and not on the Quality of Life (QOL) of the people. This must change. For sustainability and socially responsibility, businesses and industries need to pay attention to the People and the Planet, in addition to Profit (the three P's), as suggested by John Elkington.[17]

Social Inequalities and Divisions

I wish to share one other thought. Scientific and technological advances have brought us all closer in some respects. They have played a part in socio-economic divides between the "have's" and "have-nots." They have also contributed to fears, fanatic nationalism, and intense tribalism through social media.

Major divisions are seen even within nations among its own people. In countries that were under colonial rule, native people became second class citizens. Values of the dominant culture were forced on them. Pre-existent divisions and battles between groups in these countries played into the hands of the colonial powers.

How are these divisions and conflicts playing out in India and US, two countries I know something about?

India has received people from other lands from early in its civilization. Leaving aside the question of migration of pre-Vedic people, we know of immigrants from the land of Canaan in 56 BCE soon after the second destruction of the Temple in Jerusalem. Zoroastrians probably came to India in the 8th century. There was trade between the Roman Empire and the southern parts of India. There was a Roman settlement in the southern parts of India. The earliest Christian to arrive in India was Saint Thomas in 56 CE. Earliest mosque known to have existed in India goes to the lifetime of the Prophet himself. In fact, when the Christian missionaries and Arab traders came to India in the 1400s, they found all these groups and more. All

---

[17] *What is Triple Bottom Line?* Executive Factsheet. https://www.hec.edu

of them had names for their groups. There was no name for the native people, who followed Vedic texts. They were called the Hindus. India has assimilated the best of all its diverse religions, languages, and cultures. Society has thrived on diversity and tolerance. The Indian Constitution enshrines it.

The Unites States of America has also thrived on diversity. The Statue of Liberty is a symbol of welcome for all. In the words of Emma Lazarus, the Lady is saying: "Give me your tired, your poor, / Your huddled masses yearning to breathe free." Because of the freedom its constitution provided for all, it was and is a magnet for the brightest and the best from all over the world. In its short, six hundred years of history, its people, most of them immigrants have enriched the lives of all the people, all over the world. It has also been a beacon of hope for the downtrodden and the oppressed. We have people originating from every nation on earth on this land.

All is not well, however. There is a trend towards parochialism, tribalism, and nationalism all over the world. India and US are no exceptions. There are many conflicts around the world arising out of past injustices committed by one group of people over another. Now people who were oppressed in the past, based on religion, caste, ethnic group, color of skin or language or for whatever other reason, are clamoring for justice. But the current descendants of oppressors of the past cannot repair the actions of their ancestors. The current descendants of the oppressed and the enslaved cannot keep suffering the same injustices forever.

Need for Reconciliation

Unless there is genuine repentance for our past injustices and reconciliation, I do not know how all of you of the future generations can live in peace and harmony.

Reconciliation, to me, is a spiritual process. It should be more than a legal process or a monetary compensation. I would argue that speaking of monetary compensation is disrespectful of the lives that were lost in pain and suffering.

Reconciliation requires genuine repentance and acknowledgement by one party for the past injustices. It requires the offended party to genuinely forgive the injustices suffered by their ancestors. This should be followed by meaningful reforms. This entire process should be non-violent done with humility, loving-kindness, and compassion.

So, what is the message?

At present, our civilization is facing two major challenges:

1. Climate-related disasters and disappearance of species.
2. Dangers related to irrational group behavior rooted in the weakness of human biology and social media.

The future of the planet and of the people is in urgent need of stabilizing actions by the current inhabitants of this planet.

12. Individuality, personal happiness, and legality go together. Cooperation, collective welfare, and morality go together.

What are the current needs of our civilization?

My simple answer to this question is: cooperation, collective welfare, common good, and common purpose.

During the recent pandemic I was thinking about the stresses piling up on common folks, and particularly on the poor and the vulnerable, all over the world. I realized how vulnerable we are. We humans depend on each other for survival. This virus does not care where you are from, whether you are a male or a female, white or person of color, or whatever category you want to pigeonhole people into.

Some lessons I learned were: 1) the recognition of who the essential workers in a society are; 2) that most of these workers are women and minorities; 3) this pandemic is taking an undue toll among the poor; 4) the socio-economic divide in society is made glaringly obvious by this small virus; and 5) the most altruistic people of the society are the front-line essential workers. We need to learn from them.

When I thought about things that need our attention, I realized that listing problems and writing solutions are not adequate, if I do not envision the kind of society I want to live in and what I want the future to be for my children and grandchildren.

Several factors during the past few decades have driven our civilization to a critical point in history. Scientific developments, technological advances, and education of professionals in every field have contributed immensely to uplifting millions around the world out of poverty. Rewards for contribution to society as well as encouragement and recognition of individuals for such contributions have benefitted humanity in general. More recent developments, including rapid travel and instant communication, have brought peoples of the world together more than ever before.

At the same time, the social and economic divides have become wider. All kinds of -*isms* are driving people into corners and polar positions, partly due to social media. In addition to contending with rapid spread of infections such as Covid-19, we now have to deal with endemic "mental viruses" such as racial bias, gender bias, color bias, caste bias, etc., and the "viral transmission" (Infodemics) of fake news, conspiracy theories, and rumors via the social media.

Civilization is currently dominated by:

1. commodification, commercialization, and competition that "water the seeds" of desire, greed, ego, and aggressiveness;
2. advertisements, movies, computer games, and social media that evoke more desires, wants, and passion; and
3. political discourse that is rude, uncivil, and divisive, leading to hate and fear.

I would like to see these three trends balanced with love, compassion, humility, justice, and harmony.

This is a suitable time for civilization to rethink its purpose, refocus on priorities, and reimagine the future. What would a broad and bold vision, which will appeal to most people, look like?

Here is a personal point of view: Humanity has reaped the fruits of socio-political philosophy emphasizing primacy of the individual (personal effort and success—in other words, competition), pursuit of happiness, and legal rights. It is time to balance them with a system that emphasizes common purposes of collective welfare, cooperation, spiritual happiness, morality, and ethics. Robin Kimmerer would say: "Flourishing is mutual".

We live in a period in history when competition and pursuit of happiness are overemphasized. When we compete, the emphasis is on the individual, and on winning. To quote the famous football coach Vince Lombardi: "Winning is not everything. It is the only thing." This leads to an attitude of winning at any cost.

In our desire to "win at all costs," some of us are likely to use unfair methods or try to cheat, lie, or steal to win. Even if we win "fair and square," someone else loses. If we win by unfair means, the loser will wait for his/her chance to get even. There will be unhappiness and disharmony.

Most of the competition is for physical possessions, fame, and fortune in the "pursuit of happiness." The word "happiness" is most often connected in the minds of most people with material happiness. Competition begets more competition because everyone wants to get what the other person has and wants to build a house bigger than the other. More emphasis on individual happiness and individual success leads us to our own private islands. It leads to social isolation, suffering, sadness, depression, jealousy, and anger in one group. It leads to anxiety, restlessness, fear, and moral torpor in another group. There is misery all around. Social media is accelerating these trends.

On further thinking, I believe that one other cause for social disharmony is the primacy given to legality over morality and ethics. In settling disputes coming out of competition—conflicts in individual human rights and property rights and injury caused by relentless pursuit of profits and happiness—the current ethos among several people, particularly in business and politics, seems to be that if one can get away with the "fine print" of law, it is acceptable even if it is immoral. Morality and ethics do not seem to matter. To quote Alexander Solzhenitsyn:

> I have spent all my life under a communist regime, and I will tell you that a society without any objective legal scale is a terrible one indeed. But a society with no other scale but the legal one is not quite worthy of man either.

How can we escape this cycle? What are some principles to guide me to a vision for the future?

In a peaceful and just society, cooperation would have moderated competition. The word *happiness* would include collective happiness and spiritual happiness. The pursuit of individual happiness would include not only pursuit of material happiness but also happiness of others, spiritual happiness, and universal welfare.

Morality and ethics would take precedence over legality. Even if the law allows, I will not practice what the "inner light" says is immoral.

Responsibilities and duties of the individuals, organizations, and the government will be considered covenants, in which the more powerful in the transaction takes care of the welfare of the weaker participant; and not mere legal contracts, buried in small prints and disclaimers, which can be manipulated by the rich and the powerful.

Great civilizations need lofty ideals to aim for and to be guided by noble values.

13. *Sacredness seems to demand exclusivity and to breed ancestral hatred.*

> ......our insistence on historical holy lands has robbed all lands and denied their inhabitants the right to find God in their own indigenous landscapes.[18]

I thought about the association between sacredness and hatred soon after September 11, 2001, when I was praying at the St. Anthony's Cathedral at Padua, Italy. Why do we fight with each other and kill in the name of God, religion, and sacredness?

Cultural Attitude to Land

Since many disputes around the world are related to sacred sites, I wish to apply my understanding of cultural anthropology as an introduction to this essay.

As I understand it, the views and laws of the Western civilization consider land and its contents, above or below the surface, as personal property that can be owned and fenced. Laws were developed for orderly ownership of property and their use, sales, and transfers. In this worldview, the resources of the earth are for the benefit of humans and therefore it is acceptable to mine the fields, cut the trees, and dam the waters.

---

[18] J. C. Woods, *The Voices of Silence: Meditation on T. S. Eliot's Four Quartets*

When the Western colonizers with this attitude arrived, indigenous people everywhere in the world were caught by surprise. Initially, they gave the new arrivals land to grow or graze animals because according to them, the land belongs to everyone, and it is meant to be shared. But, as one New Zealander told me, the natives did not know that the newcomers would build a fence around the land given to them and consider it their personal property, a concept alien to their culture.

In her book *Braiding Sweetgrass,* Robin Wall Kimmerer poignantly writes that her ancestors from the Potawatomi Nation were offered the right to own their own property as individuals only if they agreed to "surrender their allegiance to land held in common."

Of course, there will be conflicts if usable land is considered common property. Indigenous cultures also had their own ideas of what land property means and how it should be used in a sustainable manner for collective welfare.

The Western civilization considers land and its contents as a personal property and can be owned and used (or exploited) for the benefit of the owner. Most indigenous cultures consider everything on earth as sacred and meant to be used for collective welfare. These cultures feel a sense of respect for earth and everything in it, and a sense of mutual responsibility towards everything on this earth. Their cultural approach is "give-and-take," a reciprocal one. In Kimmerer's words, it is a state of "mutual flourishing."

Mother Earth gives us gifts. Gifts create mutual bonding. Gifts come with responsibilities. That includes taking care of the Earth and the plants and the animals, all the resources of the earth and sharing the gifts.

The focus of indigenous people is on living with nature and sustainable use of the resources. The focus of the western culture is living in control of nature and use the land and its contents for good purpose. In modern consumer society, this means unsustainable use of earth's resources. We are already seeing the negative aspects of this view of earth and its resources.

Fortunately, the voices of the indigenous people are being heard. For example, the elders of the island-nation of Palau have strict rules on fishing in coral reefs to allow for replenishment of fish that live in these corals. In Oregon, the leaders of the Indigenous people were able to remove a dam so that salmons can return to their spawning ground.

Cultural attitudes to science, combined with the belief that all the resources of the earth were made for humans to enjoy, use and flourish made it possible for Western cultures to develop many new technologies. These technologies obviously benefit people living in all parts of the world.

Unfortunately, many countries which were under colonial rule during the period of rapid development of technologies in the West are now independent. All their people want to flourish and want the same level of comfort and the gadgets that go with those comforts. Thanks to science and technology, population in these countries have also increased due to falling death rates and longer life span. With increasing population there is an increasing demand for more goods. This in turn puts more strain on the earth's dwindling resources.

It is a good time to rethink our relationship with earth and how we use earth's resources. It is time consider Mother Earth as our common sacred land.

What is meant by sacred? What makes something sacred?

Conflicts start once a site is designated sacred for a particular group, and what is worse, they continue for generations. In India, Ayodhya is considered the birthplace of

Lord Rama. Therefore, it is a holy site. Historically there is adequate documentation to show that Islamic invaders destroyed temples in India. During their reign, they built a mosque at the site where there was a Hindu temple that was destroyed. After independence, the Hindus wanted their old sacred site restored and wanted to build a temple for Rama. This issue got litigated and went up to the Supreme Court of India.

In Jerusalem, when the old Jewish temple was destroyed in the first century, Jerusalem was taken over by the Roman Empire and became a holy site for the Christians, since Jesus lived and taught in that general area. Then came the Islamic conquest in the seventh century, and Jerusalem was under Turkish control till 1918 when the British conquered the Ottoman empire. It so happens that Jerusalem is also claimed by Islam since Prophet Mohamed is considered to have ascended to heaven from the Rock of the Dome. Now it is part of Israel.

Current conflicts involve religions arising out of the same source. That seems to be the power of sacredness—dividing people, inciting ancestral hatred, violence, and perpetual war in the name of God and religion.

Many atrocities have been committed over the centuries in the name of sacred sites, symbols, and scriptures. All traditions have their own sacred symbols and scriptures, which when viewed with an open mind, show that they teach the same universal values. Understanding the meaning behind another's sacred symbols is the first step towards tolerance and acceptance. Such an understanding and tolerance will reduce much of cruelty by man against man, particularly in the name of religion.

No object is intrinsically sacred or profane until it is given that status by society. It depends upon whether we emphasize the utilitarian value of the object or its intrinsic significance, which is beyond its material value. The word "sacred" implies an item that has deep emotional value that cannot be measured against monetary values. Sacred values are not for sale. Some objects and values are so special for the faithful, that they think it is worth sacrificing one's life for the sake of those objects and values.

Religious communities cherish their sacred symbols and activities because their ancestors had given specific significance to those symbols and activities as part of their tradition, religious worship, and rituals. Attacks on sacred religious symbols, icons, and figures have been the origins of many wars and loss of life. Therefore, the concept of sacredness has become a subject for deep academic study in recent years.

Looking at history and the current scene, sacredness seems to demand exclusivity. Sacredness seems to breed ancestral hatreds. Sacredness seems to take on special meaning when it is challenged. People fight for the sacred object with greater intensity when it is challenged.

So-called "sacred wars" between religions have been going on for centuries, long after the original clashes took place. My great-great grandfather insulted your great-great grandfather. They fought. Things have changed since then. Why are we fighting still?

Because sacredness breeds ancestral hatreds.

The word "scripture" is invariably connected with the concept of divine origin and hence its sacredness. The Bible is sacred for the Christians, The Torah for the Jews, the Qur'an for the Muslims, the Vedas for the Hindus. Prophets from every tradition say that their scripture was revealed to them by God. Such a statement certainly gives the scripture a special place in the minds of the followers. Jerusalem is sacred for the Jews, Bethlehem for the Christians, Mecca for the Muslims, and Varanasi for the Hindus. In other words, sacredness brings exclusivity.

But, what about the scriptures revealed to other prophets in other parts of the world? What about places sacred for other groups of people, including the indigenous people for whom the land they live on is sacred? Kauffman says in his book *Reinventing the Sacred*:

> Think of all the gods and the God that humanity has cleaved to. Each has told its believers what is sacred. Whatever your own beliefs, what are we to make of these other beliefs? Either we all worship the same real and supernatural God in different names, or these gods and God are our own invented symbols.

However, scriptures themselves are no substitute for morality. Buddha said: "As the wise test gold by burning, cutting and rubbing, so are you to accept my words after examining them and not merely out of regards for me."

In the Bible, Psalm 19:27 states: "Stop listening to teachings that contradict what you know is right." Another passage from the Bible (Thessalonians 3:13) says: "Do not stifle the spirit. Test everything; retain what is good."

Adi Sankara or Shankaracharya is one of the foremost spiritual thinkers, philosopher, poet, and a saintly figure from the eighth-century India. He said: *"gnaapakam hi shastram na thu kaarakam...,"* which translates to "Scriptures are for keeping you informed (of eternal Truths) and not for issuing commands."

He added: "Veda cannot be an authority as against observed facts... Even if a hundred Vedic texts declare that fire is cold, they cannot become an authority on this point."

Reframing Conflicts around the Sacred

People defend their sacred objects with greater passion when challenged. Appeal to sacred values can motivate both war and peace. Political leaders exploit this weakness by using sacred values to mobilize people to action or to convert people to accept their policies.

Atran and Axelrod[19] offer several ideas to help reframe issues involving conflicts in sacred values. The most important step is demonstrating respect for the views of the other party and apologizing for what they sincerely regret.

Atran and Axelrod noted that making symbolic concessions of no apparent material benefit may open the way for dialogue and resolution of what seems to be irresolvable conflict. Material offers and monetary offers in matters of sacred values will be considered as insults and only lead to further estrangement.

On the other hand, a sincere apology, apology for what the party sincerely regrets, can open the way for future discussions on resolution of conflicts. Though apologies in conflicts may not by themselves be deal-makers, they may lead to facilitating political compromises. During discussion on political compromises, material transactions can be considered without being considered insulting.

Atran and Axelrod also suggest several methods to overcome barriers to communication by refining and redefining sacred values to exclude outmoded claims, reframing the contexts, and reframing responsibility. For example, it should be possible to say that we need to be careful not to admit convicted criminals from other countries entering our country illegally, instead of calling all immigrants as criminals.

---

19 Atran and Axelrod, 2008

So, what is the message?

We need the sacred in our lives. We can reap the benefits of the sacred if we hold them with an understanding of the universal values they represent, rather than allow them to breed hatred and division.

14. Universal moral rules (dharma) must be based on rationality, impartiality, universality and some flexibility.

I was sitting inside the Cathedral of St. Anthony of Padova in Italy soon after 9/11 and was reflecting on the senseless cruelty committed on innocent people. I was reflecting on the goodness of heart of so many who came to help those who were affected. It was then I sensed a need for a moral system applicable to all of humanity, a system any rational person will understand, accept, and follow, irrespective of his or her religion or culture. It should not be a Christian morality, Jewish morality, Islamic morality, Hindu morality, Jain morality or Buddhist morality. It should be universal morality.

The world is shrinking, thanks to information technology and easy international travels. There seems to be more migration than ever because of economic and political factors. Racial and cultural mixes are more common now; but tensions are also high. This is a suitable time to think about a universal moral system to bring about greater tolerance, harmony, and universal justice. I borrowed the term "Universal Moral System" from the writing of Prof. Bernard Gert,[20] who has done extensive research in moral philosophy.

Can we develop a new set of universal moral rules (*dharma*) for the 21st century? (The word *dharma* is a Sanskrit

---

[20] Gert, 1988

word which refers ultimately to morals and ethics.) Here is why I think this is necessary and is possible.

The era of enlightenment (also called the Age of Reason), starting in the eighteenth century in Europe, emphasized reason and science over blind faith and superstitions. The power of reasoning and questioning enabled by this cultural movement liberated individual human beings to develop to their fullest potential. Scientific and technological developments have increased quality of life in some parts of the world. But they have also increased the material needs of individuals with competition for limited resources and consequent inequalities. Socio-economic divides are creating conflicts around the globe.

Individualism and Morality

Individuals endowed with freedom to do what they please and resources to get what they want (not necessarily what they need) tend to forget that others also have human needs and aspirations. When individual achievements define who you are, what you can get, and what you can get away with, competition becomes a part of the societal fabric.

When primacy of the individual is overemphasized, each one tries to defend his or her boundary. Each one becomes an island. We forget that we are interconnected. Instead of connecting and cooperating, we resort to adversarial legal relationship. But emphasis on individual freedom without emphasis on associated responsibilities, and emphasis on legal relationship at the cost of moral relationship leads to injustice, associated conflicts, and weakening of the society. Recognition of the common web of life and of interconnectedness is more likely to lead to a harmonious society and happiness for all.

Business and Morality

The emergence of private enterprise, commerce, and industry add to the complexity. One enters business to make money. If that is not the motive, why would anyone want to do business? There is nothing inherently wrong with business and reasonable profit. Indeed, we need them for a functioning society. Businesses give livelihood to many and serve the needs of people. But the problem is when the owners and leaders become greedy, focus on their individual success and profits, and forget the welfare of the society. They forget that greediness makes them cheat and thus lose the trust of the people. Profit motive is not the problem. Greed and misuse of trust are the problems. This happens because business owners sometimes forget that they are part of the fabric of the society, and they have an unwritten, moral contract with the people.

The focus in the past two or three centuries has been on individual liberty, commerce, and reliance on legal contracts to protect the weak. Now it is time for all of us to emphasize the importance of personal virtue and moral responsibility of the individual to maintain the welfare of all and thus strengthen the society. If every one of us recognize our responsibility to others in the society and develop our own "inner policeman," we will have less need for an "outer policeman."

Laws, Rules, and Universal Moral Codes

When individual needs and roles intersect with the needs and roles of others, we need boundaries and acceptable rules of conduct. We develop laws for this purpose. Laws applied with mercy and impartiality are necessary for a civil society. In addition, we need a new set of guidelines in the form of a universal moral system as proposed by Prof. Gert for developing our individual inner controls.

We do not have to invent new rules. All religions already enshrine a set of moral values and codes of conduct. But they are not universal. They are specific to those professing that religion. Different religions have different sets of values, and all supposedly given by God. "God-given" is not an adequate reason to insist on following a rule, since different people follow different gods. And what to do with atheists who deny the existence of God? If God of one group allows the followers to commit an immoral act against another group, should one do it? Some with intense faith will say "yes," but for an impartial person or for one who does not follow that faith, it will be an immoral act. That is why we need a universal system of morality based on rationality and therefore acceptable to all.

Moral philosophy is a complicated subject and I do not wish to profess depth of knowledge. I want to take a common-sense view of morality and look for a set of moral rules acceptable to all of humanity. Given my personal background I first looked at the concept of dharma in the Indian tradition.

Dharma

The word *dharma* is a Sanskrit word. The root syllable is *dhru*, to support. Support what? The word *dharma* represents virtues that support living in harmony with oneself, with others (society), and with nature. The root word *dhru* also means "that which sustains" (law and order) and "that which controls" the human weakness. *Dharma* is a collective term for a code of conduct, covering every sphere of human activity in relation to other individuals and the society. Another feature of this concept of dharma in the Indian philosophy is its flexibility, a controversial aspect I will discuss later.

Dharma for the twenty-first century, as I envision, will consist of rules of conduct to be practiced by every individual that support human virtues, sustain law and order, and control human weakness. It will encompass justice, morality, duty, righteous conduct, charity, and law, all rolled into one. This set of rules must be able to operate on its own logical merit, and not get mixed with theological, political, or legal concepts and dogmas. The rules will have to be simple, self-evident, flexible, understandable, and acceptable to any reasonable person.

Gert's Rules

Such a system can be found in the writings of Prof. Gert, a professor of intellectual and moral philosophy, who considers morality "as a public system that applies to all rational person." In the Preface to the first edition of his book, he states: "If morality is limited to its proper sphere, then one can expect almost complete agreement among rational men on all questions of morality."

Prof. Gert's rules of moral conduct are simple and self-evident. They are based on rationality, impartiality, and universality. In addition, this system also suggests rules to allow for some flexibility.

I leave it to the readers to review the book on *Morality—A New Justification of the Moral Rules* to understand the extensive philosophical and logical reasons behind the rules he has listed in the book. For our purposes, I outline some important points from this book.

The goal of any moral system (composed of moral rules) should be to minimize suffering caused by acts that harm others. It should explain and justify its component parts. It should also establish explicit procedures for determining the basis of these moral rules and, also of procedures for determining morally acceptable violations of the moral rules.

The core of the universal moral system will apply to all rational people in their behavior towards others in whichever part of the world they live, irrespective of their culture or religion. Impartiality, as outlined by Prof. Gert, specifies not only who is being impartial, but also toward what group one is impartial and in what aspect. Impartiality is particularly important when violations for specific circumstances are defined as part of these rules.

Based on these principles, Prof. Gert listed five major and five minor moral rules. The five majors are: Do not cause death; do not cause pain; do not cause loss of ability; do not cause loss of freedom; do not cause loss of pleasure. The other five are: Do not deceive; keep your promise; do not cheat; obey the law; and do your duty. These rules are based on sound theoretical reasoning.

Breaking the Rules

These are universal principles well-known to adherents of different traditions since they are already part of all the existent religion-based moral systems. However, there will be occasions when one of these rules may have to be broken. One must then choose between difficult alternatives as told in the following story from the ancient Indian epic, the *Mahabharata*.

This is the story of King Sibi. Sibi was a noble and just king who gave protection to the weak and downtrodden. One day, a hawk was chasing a pigeon for its food. The pigeon landed on King Sibi's lap asking for protection. The hawk arrived soon after and asked King Sibi to let go of the pigeon so he could have his food for the day. Sibi refused to let go and the discussion that ensued between King Sibi and the hawk is a treatise on what virtue is and how one decides what is right, when there are competing interests.

"A king's duty is to give protection to whoever comes asking for one," says Sibi and refuses to give up the pigeon.

The hawk says: "How can you do this deed unworthy of you. I am hungry and you are withholding my food. You think you are practicing virtue; but in fact, you are not."

The king replies: "This pigeon is afraid of being eaten and has come to me asking to save its life. Why do you think that allowing him to be eaten by you is a greater virtue?"

The hawk says: "It is from food that all beings derive their life and get sustained. One cannot live long without food. If deprived of food, I will die. If I die, members of my family will also perish. By protecting this single pigeon, you jeopardize many other lives. A virtue that stands in the way of another is certainly not a virtue but is unrighteousness. After comparing opposing virtues, and weighing their comparative merits, one should act in a way not opposed to some other virtue. O king, strike a balance between virtues and follow a path which is more righteous."

The king says that forsaking one who has sought asylum is not virtuous. And says: "You are hungry. You need food. There are so many other options—an ox, a deer, a buffalo. Ask me for one and I will get you."

The hawk says: "I do not eat a fox or an ox. A pigeon is my natural food. That is way nature has ordained things."

The king refuses and says: "Ask for any other thing—but not this pigeon."

The hawk asks for the king's flesh. The king takes a piece of his own flesh from his thigh and gives it to the hawk. The hawk and the pigeon declare themselves to be Divine emissaries and praise the greatness and magnanimity of King Sibi.

Flexible Systems

Life is full of moral dilemmas like this story and other situations where there is no simple "right" or "wrong" solution. This is why it is difficult to develop and adopt a universal moral system which is too rigid. As pointed out by Prof. Gert, some rational people may not want these rules to be obeyed irrespective of the circumstances. There are circumstances when one of these rules may have to be broken. Best example is telling a lie to save a life. In other words, there should be scope for exceptions. Such flexibility is a basic feature of dharma as written in ancient Indian texts.

Interestingly this idea of exception to moral rules was one of the recurrent themes in the *Mahabharata*. The entire epic is a study in morals and ethics. It teaches primarily about the immorality of cheating and lying. There are also episodes in this epic outlining conditions under which it is acceptable, and indeed may be necessary, to utter a lie or steal. In fact, one branch of dharma is called *aapad dharma*, which includes rules of conduct when in danger.

Here is an example from the *Mahabharata*. Draupadi, the wife of the Pandavas, lists conditions under which it is acceptable for a king (ruler) to break the rule of "Do not kill." They are:

> When someone is ready to kill you or one of your people; one who is trying to poison you; one who kills others for no reason; and one who is trying to take away your wife.

Remember that these exceptions were spelled out specifically for a ruler and in the remote past.

This is where Prof. Gert's recommendation on how violations of accepted moral rules should be defined aligns with the ancient concept of Dharma. In recognition of this reality, Prof. Gert wrote that "one cannot guarantee completely impartial following of moral rules unless violations are allowed", but such violations can be allowed "only when they are determined by a procedure that is known by and acceptable to all moral agents." He also said that justified violations must be "publicly allowed." Finally, "moral impartiality requires that one never violate a moral rule unless one can advocate that such violation be publicly allowed, which requires that it be understood and could be accepted by all rational persons."

Prof. Gert suggested that exceptions also be based on the same principles as the moral rules, namely impartiality, rationality, and universality. When applied, the exception should not favor one group over another. The answer should be the same when the details of the circumstances are given, irrespective of the person who broke the rule. In Prof. Gert's words: "one must guarantee that no one will be influenced by who benefits or is hurt by what counts as the same circumstances."

This feature of allowance for violation is the most difficult part to develop in such a way that these rules can be accepted universally. But it is worth a try.

15. Individuals can have conscience, not institutions and corporations.

We discussed consciousness in an earlier essay as a sense of awareness of oneself and of the world around us. Now we discuss conscience, which is a moral sense with a set of principles and values which guide our actions. Individuals can have conscience. Collectives cannot.

Please let me give a brief introduction to this essay, in which I explain the need for a "cabinet of the collective conscience." I wrote this piece almost thirty years back. After a review by a reputed journalist, I sent this to two major newspapers to be published as a "Letter to the Editor." Obviously, this essay was rejected and was buried in my files for several years. I think that the ideas suggested in this essay are more valid now than ever before and therefore decided to revive it here.

We live in a tumultuous period in history.

Science is making rapid advances in every field that test human capacity for ethical decision-making. Information technology is breaking barriers and testing the limits of freedom. Artificial Intelligence and natural language processing applications are already causing anxieties about their impact on the society. Science is wedded to objectivity and data and is unable to bridge the gap between human abilities, human needs, and the human psyche.

At the same time, and probably because of our inability to face these challenges created by science and technology, some are retreating into old shells and refuse to accept current realities. These folks refuse to use objective data to make reasoned decisions. They are prepared to even refuse to teach children how to reason.

The task of being a leader of a nation in such times requires both knowledge and sensitivity. They need advice from both technical experts and wise elders. That is why I propose that leaders of nations take counsel from an unofficial cabinet, representing the conscience of the people, before making major decisions. This "Cabinet of Collective Conscience" (CCC) will ideally consist of a wise elder, a poet, and a humorist.

This is not a novel idea. We learn from the history books that wise leaders of the past have used such counsel.

At present, there are technical experts and specialists in senior positions in all branches of the government to advise the leader of every nation (president or prime minister) on complex issues. We need their knowledge for making decisions in this complex world. National leaders, such as our president, will have to take advice from technical experts before they make decisions on key issues. Decisions must be based on facts, primarily.

However, specialists and experts often see the tree but cannot imagine the forest. Given the complexity of modern societies, solutions to problems involving people and nations require more than technical knowledge. Perceptions, emotions, values, and aspirations of people need to be considered.

Thoughtful physicians and good managers are aware of this need for both technical expertise and sensitivity to achieve superior results. They know that solutions based on scientific knowledge alone, that do not consider the feelings and the values of the people involved, are not likely to lead to satisfactory outcomes.

This is particularly true in the governance of nations. Leaders need a great fund of knowledge. They also need humility, an open mind to take counsel from experts in the field and from those who are known for being in touch with the feelings, values, and aspirations of the average person.

Hopefully, the leader of every nation will appoint a national repository of collective conscience of its people from which to take counsel. This advisory group, the Cabinet of the Collective Conscience, will consist of three individuals who have a feel for and give expression to common voices of humanity.

The first is a wise elder who is trusted by society, who is known to speak his/her conscience, and who cares for the welfare of the people of his country and of the world. I am thinking of people in the caliber of a Mahatma Gandhi, a Nelson Mandela, or a Martin Luther King.

The second is a poet. Poets see things from an aesthetic point of view. They look at the universal dimensions of the world.

I am thinking of someone like Robert Frost who said:

> We dance round the ring and suppose;
> But the Secret sits in the middle and knows

or like Maya Angelou who said:
> I've learned that people will forget what you said,
> and people will forget what you've done, but
> people will never forget how you made them feel.

Finally, we need a humorist who can call the king "naked" when he indeed is! A comedian, a court jester, can say the truth in such a way that makes everyone, including the king, laugh. Using deft humor, he will have the power to point out the incongruities and hypocrisy of the powerful, just as Will Rogers did a century back.

How should such a cabinet be chosen? The best option is for the public to choose. In this era of interactive communication, it is possible for people to vote via internet. I recommend that a concise list be prepared by respected organizations, such as the Library of Congress and the American Academy of Arts and Letters, and that the people select the final panel from that list.

The three chosen ones would then represent the voices and the aspirations of the people. They will be the canaries of our subterranean minds! They do not have to tell us what their advice to the president was, just as the president need not take their advice. However, the national leader may choose to tell the people the advice he/she received, after the decision is made, particularly if their advice was different from the technical advice. An annual forum, with public participation, where these three express their thoughts on some of the pressing issues of the society may be helpful to both the leaders and the public.

Before making grand decisions, our president and other world leaders will be expected to consult members of their country's Cabinet of the Collective Conscience. These gurus will not have the final say, of course. Still, an open-minded leader will be able to hear the weaknesses, short-sightedness, and incongruities in decisions made solely based on technical advice and his/her own political bias. More importantly, the leader will have the advantage of checking his/her own political beliefs and the cold logic of technical experts with the voices of the humanity, thus making the final decisions practical and of longer-lasting value.

16. We need a new world mythology and shared sacred sites...

This aphorism was inspired by the writings of Joseph Campbell and Scott Momaday.

The human mind is an amazing creation of nature. It demands an answer for the mystery of its own existence and even attempts to provide an answer. Thanks to my medical profession and my own interest in diagnostic challenges, I have been thinking about the mind and its mechanisms for most of my adult life. In addition, immersion in meditation extended the realm of my thinking to another dimension. More recently, my life in a senior home has given me yet another perspective, because of contact with residents who are living with various levels of memory loss. Finally, information technology and its influence on our thinking at every level have given me an urgency to share the following thoughts.

Recognizing Real from Imaginary

The way our brains are made to function, and the way our mind works, we do not see things as they are, but the way we want them to be and the way we were taught to believe they are. We are easily fooled by our senses and blinded by our biases and prejudices. This has been so even before the arrival of the Age of Information and Information Disorder. In a world made by artificial intelligence, virtual images, imaginary money, and commodification of everything, how are we to know what is real and what is imaginary; what is the truth and what is a lie. More than ever, we are forced to learn how to recognize the real from the imaginary, truth from falsehood, and to learn to think for ourselves.

Humanity has come a long way, and thanks to the advances in science and technology in the past two- to three-hundred years, so many lives have been saved and so many have been enriched. So much more is possible. But when we look at the advances we have made and the challenges we face because of these advances, a course correction may be in order in this era of information overload and information disorder.

Harmony in the Past

Way back when, early humans lived as small tribes, very much like the few hunter-gatherers who still live in the Andaman Islands and remote regions of the Amazon River forests. Survival of the individual required being part of groups, small clans. Individuals had to give up some personal choices and freedom for the safety and survival of the group, which in turn protected the individual.

They lived in harmony with nature and respected it for what it gave. They led a more collaborative life within their clans and with the flora and fauna around them. They were better connected with others and with nature and were aware of those connections, intuitively. They expressed themselves in group ceremonies, festivals, arts, and poetry. Tight community bonds kept them loyal to their group and kept them accountable for their moral and ethical conduct. Of course, all the love and kindness to fellow human beings disappeared when other clans encroached on their territory and their properties.

Later, with the arrival of agricultural economy and religious institutions, codes of conduct and rules were needed to keep peace within the community.

Rise of Individualism

Later still, with release from the demands for obedience to the religious institutions and monarchs, individuals learnt to think for themselves and express their individuality. Authorities were challenged. Individuality started flourishing. Individual curiosity and creativity led to innovations. Science flourished and led to a more reliable understanding of the universe. Technology has made it possible for more people to exit poverty and lead a safer life. But technology came with its own set of problems.

In addition, individuals and groups reaped economic benefits thanks to the organization of business models and newer policies and a legal system to protect individual property —both physical and intellectual.

Following the removal of the authority of monarchs, despots, dictators and religious heads, individuals flourished. Age of Reason started. Increased support for scholarly work and recognition for individual initiative and innovation led to rapid advances in science and technology. One outcome of excessive emphasis on the individual is that individual success and happiness have become the focus of our lives. A recent poll by the *Wall Street Journal* and the University of Chicago showed that individuals value items such as money, hard work, and self-fulfillment, which are oriented towards individuals, more than marriage and having children, patriotism, and religion, which are group oriented.

The Future

What can we do to face the future and help the future generations?

I am an optimist and care about the future generations. How do we look to the future and make it safe for our children and grandchildren?

In a free society, for freedom to last, each one of us has a responsibility to create conditions for the change. In this age of information disorder, climate crisis and consumerism, we need a new Dharma, we need skills to separate useful information from useless and harmful information, and we need to think on our own, and find our own bliss. In addition to getting an education to prepare us for making a living in this competitive world, we need education on two foundations, namely dharma (ethical and moral means for making that living) and a vision about our purpose in life.

For mutual flourishing, as Robin Kimmerer would put it, we need to change the way we are using the resources of this earth. We need to learn to use technology wisely. As pointed out earlier, we have been using earth's resources in an unsustainable manner. How do we bring about changes in our attitude to utilizations of earth's resources and the use of technology to ensure a safe, peaceful, and harmonious world for the future generation? What are some practical steps we can take to bring about those changes?

Earth's Resources

First, we need a change in attitude to how we treat earth and its resources. This starts with realizing the reality that Earth's resources are limited. We cannot continue to mine the earth, cut down forests and troll the oceans without depleting the resources. We need growth, but sustainable growth. We need a kind of growth in which everyone thrives.

Earth's resources should be used responsibly in a sustainable and equitable fashion. Technologies should be used wisely. In addition, human behavior also has to change in the way we use earth's resources and technologies. This change in attitude can happen if we can consider earth as Mother Earth and sacred, as Indigenous people do.

In a statement signed by several respected scientists, such as Freeman Dyson, Hans Bethe, and Stephen Jay Gould,[21] is the following passage:

> As scientists, many of us have had profound experiences of awe and reverence before the universe. We understand that what is regarded as sacred is more likely to be treated with care and respect. Our planetary home should be so regarded. Efforts to safeguard and cherish the environment need to be infused with a vision of the sacred.

Shared Sacred

We need a shared sacred to replace the isolated, parochial one. Scott Momaday, a Native American poet who has written an essay with the title "Re-inventing the Sacred"; and Stuart Kauffman, who wrote a book called *Reinventing the Sacred*, acknowledge items and places that are sacred to us individually or to our group. But it is an isolated or exclusive sacredness to one person or to one group. Both Kauffman and Momaday suggest that we reinvent a "shared sacred" space in addition to the isolated, parochial ones.

Joseph Campbell suggested that we use the ancient buildings and temples and cathedrals to talk to us about their spiritual information. He recommended cultural heritage tours

---

[21] Freeman Dyson, Hans Bethe, and Stephen Jay Gould. 1990

of such sites to look at the substance behind the symbols. That is one way to recognize "shared sacredness."

New Mythology

Joseph Campbell also suggested that "We need new mythology and new symbols. The old ones have lost their relevance and not their importance."

We need a new *world mythology*. That is possible if we visualize the picture of the earth our space-scientists have given us. One unit. A blue planet hanging in mid-air. It shows no borders. Only one border, between water and earth.

To develop a new mythology, we need to celebrate the sacred with a special image, a special day, special rituals, special ethics, and special prayers. The following paragraphs list my suggestions for an image, special day, rituals, ethics, and prayers.

Special Image

I suggest that we combine these ideas with those of Joseph Campbell, Scott Momaday, and Stuart Kaufmann and consider Mother Earth as "our shared sacred space." She has given her bounties for all lives to live for millennia and continues to do so. What better way to thank her than to recognize Mother Earth as our shared sacred space and reciprocate her generosity with our respect and care?

An image we can use for this universal day of gratitude and thanksgiving can be a picture of this blue planet from space. Or, a picture of the Milky Way taken by the Hubble Telescope, or picture of a supernova. Maybe all three?

Special Day

Maybe all of humanity can set aside one day a year for celebrating our shared sacred space. Instead of designating another special day, we can make Thanksgiving Day or Mother's Day special for this purpose. We have now seen our blue planet from space as humanity's only abode. Let us appreciate the special world we live in and pay our gratitude to her on that day, *all of us together*.

Rituals

Rituals to follow on that special day can be borrowed from a popular celebration in each society. Young and old can spend that day performing some sort of service and acts of gratitude, like feeding the poor, planting a tree, cleaning up the mess we have created, create a new abode for the animals we eliminated directly or indirectly.

Ethics

The Golden Rule is a good start for our renewed ethics. Love for all, compassion, peace, forgiveness, charity, humility, truth, and justice become the guiding ethical principles.

Prayers

Prayers and readings for that day can be based on teachings from personal and local traditions which emphasize universal welfare, the commonality of life, sacredness of all lives, love for all, peace, and harmony.

Rites of Passage

We need new rites of passage. It is particularly important for children entering adolescence. This should be more than a graduation party or giving them a car key or cell phone. It should be a day which the parents and children recognize as the day children have completed learning their "roots" (their traditions, history, and symbols) and start using their "wings" to explore the world with an open mind and acceptance of differences.

Benefit of the Shared Sacred Space

Knowledge of our history, sacred texts and myths gives us the *Roots*.

Knowledge of the universe through lived experience (body), emotions (heart), reason (mind) and the spirit helps us sprout our *Wings*.

The view of Mother Earth from space should convince us that we have just one earth. There are no borders between nations. It is our home. It is a shared sacred space for all of us.

My Prayer

Based on Vedic wisdom as I understand
Space is Expansive and limitless;
Time is Eternal.
They are inter-linked and make the Whole.
I am a tiny part of that Whole (called *Brahman*)
Therefore, a tiny part of that Whole (Brahman) is in me.
Aham Brahmasmi (I am Brahman) says the
    Brihadaranyaka Upanishad
Therefore, Brahman is in you, in everyone, and in every life.

We say that we want to enjoy Nature.
    But we build walls around ourselves!
We say we want "release," we want "freedom."
    But we keep ourselves prisoners of our own mind!
Let us remove the walls we built around ourselves
    To experience Nature as She is.
Let us remove the ego-personality built on the body
    by the mind
To experience the "heart and the spirit" of the Inner Self.

I offer my prayer in Buddha's words:

May you be well,
may you be safe and
may you be free from suffering.

SUGGESTED FURTHER READING

Ackerknecht, Erwin H. and Charles E. Rosenberg. 2016. *A Short History of Medicine—A Revised and Expanded Edition.* Baltimore, MD: Johns Hopkins University Press.

Athreya, Balu H. 2014. "Information in Medical Sciences." glossariumBITri. March 19. Accessed August 23, 2018. https://sites.google.com/site/glosariobitrum/glossary/information-in-medical-sciences.

Atmananda, Swami. 1964. *Sankara's Teachings in His Own Words.* Mumbai, India: Bhavan's Books.

Atran, S. and R. Axelrod. 2008. "Reframing Sacred Values." *Negotiation Journal* (Harvard) 24: 221-246.

Atran, S., R. Axelrod, and R. Davis. 2007. "Sacred Barriers to Conflict Resolution." *Science* 317: 1039-1040.

Basham, A. L. 1967. *The Wonder That Was India.* Kolkata, India: Rupa Publishers.

Beveridge. W. I. 1957. *The Art of Scientific Investigation 3rd Edition.* London: William Heinemann Publications.

Borinskaya S. A., A. I. Ermolaev, and E. I. Kolchinsky. 2019. "Lysenkoism Against Genetics: The Meeting of the Lenin All-Union Academy of Agricultural Sciences of August 1948, Its Background, Causes, and Aftermath." *Genetics.* 2019. 212(1): 1–12.

Bremermann, H. J. 1965. "Quantum Noise and Information." Fifth Berkeley Symposium on Mathematical Statistics and Probability. Berkeley, CA: University of California Press.

Bryson, B. 2004. *A Short History of Nearly Everything.* New York: Broadway Books.

Bush, Vannever. 1945. *Science the Endless Frontier.* A Report to the President by Vannevar Bush, Director of the Office of Scientific Research and Development, July 1945. Washington, D.C. United States Government Printing Office. Science the Endless Frontier (nsf.gov) (accessed December 14, 2023)

Calvino, I. 2015. *Complete Cosmicomics.* Mariner Books.

Campbell, J. 1991. *Oriental Mythology (The Masks of God).* London and New York: Penguin Books.

Campbell, J. 1981. *The Mythic Image.* Princeton. Princeton University Press.

Campbell, J. 2008. *The Hero with a Thousand Faces* (3rd Ed). Novato, CA: New World Library.

Cannon, Walter B. 1932. *The Wisdom of the Body.* New York: W.W. Norton.

Chamberlain, P. C. (1965) "The Method of Multiple Working Hypothesis." *Science.* 148, 754 – 759.

Clendening, L. 1960. *Source Book of Medical History.* Dover.

Cowell, E. B., A. E. Gough, and (Translators). 1996. *Sarva-Darshana Samgraha of Madhvacharya.* New Delhi, India: Motilal Banarsidass.

Diaz-Nafria, J., and E. Zimmermann. 2013. "Emergence and Evolution." *Triple C* 11: 13-35.

Hofstadter, D. 2007. *I am a Stange Loop.* New York: Basic Books.

Dyson F., H. Bethe, and S. J. Gould. 1990. "Preserving and Cherishing the Earth: An appeal for Joint Commission in Science and Religion" in the Global Forum on Religion and Ecology, Moscow.

Durant W. and A. Durant. 1968. *The Lessons of History*. New York: Simon and Schuster.

Eck, D. 2003. *Encountering God. A Spiritual Journey from Bozeman to Banaras—Second Edition*. Boston, MA: Beacon Press.

Eck, D. 2015. B*anaras—City of Light*. Gurgaon, India: Penguin Books.

Flexner, A. 2017. *Usefulness of Useless Knowledge*. Princeton, NJ: Princeton University Press.

Frank, Adam, Marcelo Gleiser, and Evan Thompson. 2024. *The Blind Spot: Why Science cannot ignore Human Experience*. Cambridge, Massachusetts: MIT Press,

Gert, B. 1988. *Morality: A New Justification of the Moral Rules*. Oxford, UK: Oxford University Press.

Goswami, C, L., trans. 2005. *Srimad Bhagavatha Puranam*. Gorakhpur, India: Gita Press.

Griffiths, B. 1982. *The Marriage of the East and West*. Springfield, IL: Templegate Press.

Hart, W. 2008. *The Art of Living: Vipassana Meditation*. New York: Harper One.

Huxley, A. 1944. *The Perennial Philosophy*. New York: Harper Colophon.

Kakar, S. and K. Kakar. 2007. *The Indians*. New Delhi. Penguin/Viking.

Kauffman, S. A. 2010. *Reinventing the Sacred: A New View of Science, Reason and Religion*. New York: Basic Books.

Kluckhohn, C. 1954. *Mirror for Man*. New York. Fawcett World Library for McGraw-Hill.

Levin, M. 2019. "The Computational Boundary of a "Self": Developmental Bioelectricity Drives Multicellularity and Scale-Free Cognition." *Front. Psychol.* 10:2688.doi: 10.3389/fpsyg.2019.02688

Lloyd, S. 2007. *Programming the Universe: A Quantum Computer Scientist takes on the Cosmos.* London: Vintage Books.

Meghani Z., and J. Kuzma. 2011. "The 'Revolving Door' between Regulatory Agencies and Industry: A Problem That Requires Reconceptualizing Objectivity." *Journal of Agricultural and Environmental Ethics.* 24:575–599.

Narayan, R. H. 2012. *Nyaya-Vaiseshika: The Indian Tradition of Physics.* Accessed March 26, 2014.

Percy, W. 1983. *The Message in the Bottle.* New York: Farrar, Straus and Giroux. Page 322.

Platt, J. R. 1964. "Strong Inference." *Science.* 146, 347 - 353.

Price, I. 2014. *In the Beginning. Creation Myths Across Cultures. One Truth Many Paths.* Kindle Edition.

Radhakrishnan and C. A. Moore. 1957. *A Source Book in Indian Philosophy.* Princeton, NJ: Princeton University Press.

Ramanujam, P. S. 1979. *Vyomasiva's Vaisesika.* Mysore, India: University of Mysore Press.

Rogers, C. R. 1961. *On Becoming a Person.* Boston. Houghton Mifflin.

Schrodinger, E. 2010. "What is Matter?" *Scientific American. Special Edition on Nobel Prize Winning Authors.* Vol. II. 6-10.

Smith, H. 1953. *From Fish to Philosopher.* CIBA Edition. Boston: Little, Brown & Co.

Stanford Encyclopedia of Philosophy. Accessed July 28, 2018. https://plato.stanford.edu/contents.html.

Stonier T. 1996. "Information as a basic property of the universe." *Biosystems* 38: 135-140.

Thouless, R. H. 2011. *Straight and Crooked Thinking.* London, UK: Holder and Stoughton.

Tolstoy, L. 1997. *A Calendar of Wisdom.* Edited by Sekirin. New York: Scribner.

Tolstoy, L. 2018. *What I Believe: My Religion.* London, UK: Forgotten Books.

Umpleby, S. 2007. "Physical relationship among matter, energy, and information." *Systems Research and Behavioral Science* 24, 369-372.

von Weizsäcker, C. F. 2006. *The Structure of Physics* (Translated by Biritz, H.). The Netherlands: Springer.

Vyasa. 2015. *Mahabharata.* 21st. Translated by Bibek Debroy. 10 vols. London and Goregaun, India. Penguin.

Weil, N. 2017. "Beliefs, Values, and Cultural Universals," Chapter 6. *Speaking of Culture.* Rebus Community Publishing.

ABOUT THE AUTHOR

Balu Athreya's professional career was in academic pediatrics—care of children, teaching, and research. As a pediatrician, he has always been interested in the welfare of children and their future growth and development in all dimensions. In this era of information disorder and severe climate-related events, he is concerned about the future generations and would like to see them living in a world of stability, peace, and harmony. This book is a collection of some of his thoughts towards attaining that goal.